I Know You Love Me

TO MY HUSBAND, BILL

Jean Kaiserling

I Know You Love Me
Copyright © 2024 by Jean Kaiserling

Library of Congress Control Number: 2024914669

ISBN
978-1-964982-16-8 (Paperback)
978-1-964982-17-5 (eBook)

Dedication

I dedicate this book to my husband, Bill. I want to share the sheer delight I felt each and every day from being with him. Bill and I were constantly astounded by the amount of joy and happiness we felt for one another each and every day of our lives together.

I also want to thank God for giving me such a blessing in my life. I had no idea what true happiness was until I met Bill.

And I want to dedicate this book to all the widows who— even though they travel their own route—have gone through the same journey with the loss a spouse.

Table of Contents

Acknowledgements

A big thank you to my many dear friends and family who allowed me to write about them, and who gave me such loving encouragement.

Introduction

A Storm Approaches

The Day Before: Thursday, June 18, 2009

Driving home from work, I rolled down my car windows to enjoy the wonderfully pleasant spring day in Milwaukee, Wisconsin. I began to think about what Bill and I should do that evening. He'd be working until 7:30 p.m. and would have to be back at work by 7:30 the next morning, so we wouldn't have much time. But it felt like an evening that should be enjoyed outside.

I waited for Bill to call me, as he always did, to let me know he'd be home soon. He'd want to hear if I had any ideas for the evening's dinner—eating at home, going out to eat, or bringing something home to eat. I decided to see how he'd feel about a short motorcycle ride to Fuddruckers for burgers, fries, a malt for me, and a shake for him. We'd have to go as soon as he got home, because the forecast on the evening news was calling for overnight rain.

As expected, Bill called and liked my idea. He always liked a reason for a bike ride, not caring if we chose his 1968 Bridgestone, his 1975 Honda, or "my" 2004 Harley. We called the Harley mine because my enthusiasm about it helped us decide to buy it. We had bought it on the spot a couple of years back from Gene, a friend who Bill used to work with. Gene would occasionally stop by to visit us. That day he had driven up our driveway on his Harley Sportster, asking us if we knew anyone who wanted to buy a bike. I loved the bike right away, and asked Bill if we could get it. Bill was also excited—even to the point of saying he'd sell his other Honda if we would buy this one. We quickly found ourselves on a test ride, and decided immediately we really wanted this bike. Minutes later, with checkbook in hand, we bought the Harley.

For us, a bike ride usually consisted of a short ride to get a meal or ice cream—not real hard-core bikers. Bill had mentioned many times when passing Fuddruckers that we should eat there again sometime. I usually put it off because I was the coupon queen, always in search of some sort of discount for eating out. But tonight I didn't care about that. Bill had mentioned it so many times that I knew he'd enjoy getting his wish.

As soon as he got home, we dressed in our biker clothes and jumped on our Harley for our short ride up Blue Mound Road to Fuddruckers. I insisted on wearing our helmets. I didn't always feel like wearing them, but with the warning of rain, I didn't want to take chances.

Riding to the restaurant, the temperature and breeze made for a perfect ride. I enjoyed hanging onto Bill (hugging him, really) as I always did on our rides. I knew Bill also loved that, because he'd often reach back and hold onto my leg for a while.

At the restaurant, we quickly were seated in this fifties-styled restaurant, surrounded by pictures of Elvis, the Beatles, and many other artists.

Bill knew exactly what he wanted to order, as did I. The food was so good—especially the chocolate malt I was inhaling. Our conversation was fun, as usual. Bill and I never had a problem chit-chatting with one another. We both enjoyed hearing how each other's day had gone, or any other subject that came to mind. Since I was the biggest talker and the slowest eater, Bill was used to finishing before me and listening to me gab. He never complained, and he'd always get in his share of the conversation. I started thinking again about the rain coming, so I finished my meal and we headed back outside for the ride home.

As we got outside, the weather was definitely changing. The clouds were starting to look stormy and the wind was beginning to pick up. Bill started up the bike. I was glad we weren't too far from home. As we headed back down Blue Mound Road, I started feeling a few of the first drops of rain. But I knew we were only a couple of minutes from home, so I didn't worry.

We pulled into the garage and decided to be lazy and watch some TV in bed. It took us awhile to settle in, because first I needed to feed our two black labs and take them outside.

The sky was starting to darken already, so I hurried the dogs a bit—as much as you can ever hurry a black lab. We were crazy about our dogs. Bill had named the younger nine-year-old lab Lady. As she grew older, everyone decided that must have been a mistake. Even though she was a very loving, smart dog, she was easily excited by every noise or movement and didn't think twice about plowing through anything to investigate it. And since we were never able to train her to stay in the back yard (she didn't want to run away; she just wanted us to play "catch me"), we had to keep her on a leash. Her 90-some pounds of puppyish lab would move quickly to follow or chase whatever she found, without regard to what her rope was stuck on, including chairs, bushes, or little children, so nicknames like Crazy Lady, or as my brother called her, Lady Bug, became popular.

Our other dog, ten-year-old Deogee, had been an unexpected addition to our household. A few months earlier, a man at Bill's work, Cal, sadly had needed to find a new home for his dog and asked Bill if we'd be interested. He had asked everyone he knew, and the prospect of taking her to the pound was getting closer. Bill had called me and told me the story. He didn't really want a second dog again, because it caused problems with our new hobby—traveling. But since this dog was older, he figured she wouldn't be a problem. And he knew she was a very nice dog.

I, on the other hand, was crazy about most dogs, especially another black lab. Even though I agreed we'd face the problem of having to find a place to keep our pets when traveling, I really enjoyed having two dogs. We decided to take her for the weekend and see how she did in our house and with Lady. If it didn't work out, we decided we would keep her until we found another home for her.

The next day we were introduced to Deogee. She was wonderful. No leash, calm, friendly, and the dogs got along fine. I think Bill and I decided right then and there to keep her, but we went along with the original plan of seeing how the weekend went. By the next day, we knew she was part of the family, but Bill insisted on one change. The dog was named D-O-G, pronounced as it would sound if you spelled "dog." But in going to the pet store for a new identification collar, he decided to spell her name Deogee, saying if she ever got lost, someone would probably call her Dog, and she wouldn't recognize the sound of that. Since she was an older dog, changing her name would confuse her, so we all agreed on Deogee, and she had a new home.

The dogs were fed and taken outside, and now we were all back in the house, just as the rain started. It felt good to get into bed and relax. Bill was already watching TV. We had a habit of enjoying this type of relaxation too much, because we both were late-night people, only to suffer when the alarm went off in the morning.

This night we were up even later than usual, because the rain was coming down harder now. We have very large, old maple trees, and when the wind speed increases, the leaves start whirling around the trees. Years back, our largest maple tree had fallen on the front of our house, causing $10,000 in damage (thank God for home insurance). We still had a large maple tree in the back of our house, so hearing that whirling sound always caused me to worry.

Chapter One

Calls in the Night

Day One: Friday, June 19, 2009

After listening to a weather report telling just how bad the rain was going to be, we decided we'd better try to get some sleep, as it now was around 1:00 a.m. But even with the lights off, we were both having trouble settling down. The rain was hard to ignore.

Around 1:30 in the morning the telephone rang. Even though I was still partially awake, it startled me. It took until the message machine started for me to understand the voice was from Pat, Bill's closest friend from work. I shook Bill, who must have just fallen asleep, and he also awoke with a startle.

He grabbed the phone before the message was done, and I could quickly tell from the conversation that he was being asked to come back into work because of the rain. This wasn't the first time that this had occurred.

Bill worked for the electric company. The downtown area he worked in had tunnels underneath a good part of the area. The tunnels hold steam pipes to supply hot water going into the buildings for their radiators and faucets. It was important on rainy days to make sure the water levels didn't touch the steam pipes, or they could explode. Alarms and pumps were in place, but if the rain was too hard, extra workers with extra pumps were always needed.

Bill had been called in many times through the years, but this time, even more than usual, I really dreaded hearing they wanted Bill to come in to work. Besides the rain coming down so hard, he had not had any time to sleep. And since he was also working a twelve-hour day shift the next day, I was very concerned.

I turned on the TV again to listen to more weather reports. This was an unusually hard rain for Milwaukee. The weathermen were informing the audience that many roads, and even part of the interstate, were impassable because of the rain. I became very frightened that Bill would be driving while sleepy on these treacherous roads.

As he was dressing for work I repeatedly reminded him to be careful and not use the interstate. He agreed, but I was still very worried about his drive downtown.

As he was ready to leave, I could see how tired he looked. I asked him to call me when he arrived at work. He didn't want to at first, because that would wake me up again and he was worried about me having to get up for work soon. I explained I wouldn't be able to sleep until I heard he had made it to work okay, so he agreed.

We stared at each other for a while—not quite believing how our quiet, lazy evening had so drastically changed. He stared at me with those loving eyes, and he left for work. I cried.

Clutching my pillow with the phone balanced on top of it, I continued to be especially worried. It was raining so hard, and Bill had looked so tired. I was mad at his company for asking an employee who had just worked twelve hours and had to work twelve hours the next day to be called into work in the middle of the night.

I was trying to calm down and rest when I was again startled awake. I was glad to hear the phone ringing, thinking Bill was calling me from work. I was struggling in the dark to find the right phone button to answer the phone when the message machine again clicked on. Instead of hearing Bill, it was Cal, his partner for the night—the same man who had given us our dog, Deogee. He sounded very upset and was telling me Bill had been burned and they were going to St. Mary's Hospital, the burn center. By the time I pushed the correct phone button, he had hung up. I was scared stiff. *How bad are the burns, and where are they?* I wondered worriedly.

As I rushed to get dressed, prayers were filling my head. My plan was to go straight to the hospital. I was almost ready to go when the phone rang again. This time I got it in time, and it was his friend Cal again. He sounded horrible, again saying Bill had been burned. I asked where, and he said, "All over his body."

Panic filled me completely. I told him I was leaving for the hospital right away. When I hung up I started crying uncontrollably and realized just how panicked I was. I wondered whether I'd have the ability to concentrate enough to drive. So, instead, I quickly called my best friend, Beth, who lived just a few blocks from us.

Beth had been my friend since childhood. I knew she'd understand quickly just by listening to my voice. It took me only a couple of seconds to explain what was going on, when Beth said she'd be right over. I wasn't a bit surprised. Beth was an immensely responsible person. Barely a few minutes passed before she was entering my house. We rushed to her car.

The rain was slower now, so we took the interstate—the fastest way to the downtown hospital where they had taken Bill.

I was filled with tears and prayers. We were discussing the best exit to use, since we were trying to get to the hospital as fast as possible. We did a good job and were soon pulling up to the hospital emergency room entrance.

I went inside while Beth left to look for a parking spot. Just inside the door, Cal saw me and we both started crying. We held each other. I thanked him for getting Bill there; but he was beating himself up, blaming himself for anything he felt he should have done to have prevented this from happening.

I asked at the desk if I could see Bill, but they said I'd have to wait for the nurse to come out. I sat down next to Cal just as Beth entered the ER. Cal explained to me that as soon as the employees got to work, they had been assigned partners and trucks, and they were told to go to designated tunnel entrances—no time for phone calls.

I was shocked to learn which tunnel entrance his partner was describing to me. Just a week earlier, Bill and I had gone to the Milwaukee Museum, which is attached to the courthouse parking lot. As we walked through the parking lot to the museum entrance, we had passed a round tunnel entrance in the pavement. Bill explained that was one of their tunnels. The electric company's tunnels were easy to distinguish from the sewer tunnels, because they were round.

Cal continued to explain the situation. Because of the rain, Pat, the tunnel man on duty this night, was examining several of the tunnel entrances. Only one tunnel man worked on night shift. Many of us disagreed with that. If that one man was disabled in any way, he'd be alone. It had been this way for years.

This night, the rain was causing problems throughout the system, and rain was running down the courthouse tunnel entrance so fast that Pat temporarily put a plastic cover over the entrance to slow the moving water. He then started calling workers in—he had been the original caller to our house who had awakened us.

The job of the crews being called in was to investigate the area to which they were assigned and decide on which option was best. It might be they would need additional help; it might be it was something they could examine and fix, or it might be it was something that could wait until the next day, when the full staff was working. Bill, being senior tunnel man, not surprisingly, decided to examine this tunnel. He pulled away the plastic sheet, opened the tunnel cover, and stepped down the ten-rung ladder into the area below.

Cal told me Bill was only down in the tunnel for a couple of seconds when he heard Bill screaming, and then he saw steam starting to come out of the tunnel. Cal explained later that he had no idea where the steam was coming from. He had not heard an explosion and he also knew that Bill had been in the tunnel for such a short time that he couldn't have a chance to have moved any of the valves in this part of the tunnel. Cal couldn't climb down the ladder to help Bill or he himself would be overcome by the heat. Bill was not moving and was probably in shock.

Cal decided to yell to Bill to climb up the ladder. He said Bill seemed to shake his head, as if fighting off the shock, and started the climb up the ladder. Bill was an extremely strong guy, but under these conditions, his partner was amazed he was still able to climb the ladder. Bill stood before his partner, his entire body burned.

Even though Bill had to be in shock and extreme pain, he stopped, looked at his partner, and said, "Call Jean." Bill then pulled out his wallet and gave it to Cal. Then, as the pain must have overcome him, he started walking fast down the street. His partner caught up to him, got him into the truck, and started driving down the block to a fire station. This is when Cal made his first call to me, the call that I was unable to answer due to the darkness and not being able to find the right button on the phone.

Cal said the firefighters immediately worked on Bill and then drove him to nearby St. Mary's burn center. Then Cal made the second call to me.

As I listened to the story, my hopes kept my panic down. I kept telling myself that the fast action of the firefighters and the quick arrival at the burn center had to be positive news. I knew the burns had to be very dangerous; but he was being treated by top burn specialists. Bill was a big, strong guy, and I kept telling myself he'd be fighting for his life.

I was so scared, and constantly praying, when the nurse came out of Bill's ER room. He explained to me the severity of the wounds, but told me they had been able to insert the breathing tube just before Bill's throat swelled shut. This was so essential that I told myself it was a miracle, and another good sign of his chances at recovery. The nurse continued, telling me what dangerous burns Bill had, and that I should prepare myself for what Bill would look like. Again I panicked. I was afraid Bill's face may have such severe burns that I wouldn't recognize him.

I quickly followed the nurse into the room and felt relieved that I could recognize Bill. It looked like his face had severe sunburn. I went straight to his side. The nurses told me his inner ears had not suffered damage, so he should be able to hear me.

The moment I spoke, that was confirmed. Bill's head turned toward me but his eyes were already swollen, so he couldn't open them. He started moving some, so the nurses tried to hold him still.

I quickly told him I loved him and that he shouldn't worry—he was being taken care of. He looked to be in horrible pain, but the nurses explained his vitals needed to be monitored first, before they could give him more pain medication.

They also explained I'd need to go to a waiting room on the burn unit floor while they continued to work on Bill.

I hated to leave his side, but I told Bill I'd see him in a little while. Before I left the room, I told him over and over that I loved him.

Again, Cal and I cried and hugged. His partner had to leave to go back to work. A nurse walked Beth and me to the elevators that took us upstairs. Another nurse showed us a small, private, waiting area and left. We sat in shock and tears, waiting for the next step. Beth kept reminding me how strong Bill was, and that I also needed to be strong.

A new nurse soon came into the room and told me to tell her that I wouldn't speak to any reporters, and none should be allowed into the burn unit. I found it strange how she stated this, but once I repeated what she had told me to say, she let me know how important it was to do that. Otherwise, reporters would be calling and entering the area. They would soon know Bill's name and our home address and I could become surrounded by news staff. She said the accident would be on the news and it was better he wasn't named, or people could start showing up at my house. I thanked the nurse for this information.

The nurse let me know I'd be waiting for some time, as they had a lot of work to complete before I could see Bill again. Beth and I decided we needed to call the family, so I called Billy, Bill's son, with the news, and asked him to spread the news to the rest of the family. Bill had three children and two brothers, and they would all want to be here.

Beth told me she had to go move her car, but I told her to go home, because the family would be coming and it sounded like I'd be waiting for a while. She left, telling me to call her later.

Now alone, I stared at the walls, praying while crying.

A while later, a nurse entered the waiting room. She said a representative from the electric company was here to see me. I wasn't too happy about that, but I said okay and the nurse let her in.

I don't remember what area of the company she said she was from, but she started talking to me. I mostly stared at her, wishing she'd go away, already knowing I hated that company and didn't especially feel like listening to her. She soon ran out of things to say, and said she'd sit with me. I didn't especially like that idea either, but I didn't have the heart to tell her to go away. I thought she probably meant well.

We sat for a while and then the children arrived. In reality they weren't children anymore, but grown adults. Shannon was the eldest, then Billy, and then Julie. As we hugged and cried, I told the electric company lady that she could leave, since the family was here; and she agreed.

The children and I sat and cried together for a while, until finally another nurse came to tell me I could come into Bill's room. The kids would take care of calling Bill's brothers and my brother.

I quickly learned the protocol on what to do before entering a burn patient's room. The unit had an area with a sink to thoroughly wash our arms and hands. Then we had to put on a gown and gloves. I was surprised I didn't need to put on a hair covering and a mask.

The area was an ICU unit with separate patients' rooms that curved around the nurses' area. I was then escorted to Bill's room.

As I entered his room I was shocked at the change in Bill's appearance after such a short time. His face and body had swollen immensely. His face was so round he looked like a balloon. His lips were not only swollen, but extremely red. I fought back tears and got to his side at once. Once again, when he heard my voice he started struggling, which worried the nurses. He was in so much pain, but they said they still had to wait awhile before giving him any more drugs, explaining to me his vitals had to be in better control.

I barely understood their message to me at the time, as I was feeling the shock of all of this myself. Bill was trying to talk and he was fighting with the breathing tube. I knew he was trying to tell me something, but he couldn't. I kept telling him I loved him, but he wasn't calming down. I finally realized what Bill wanted. I again told him I loved him, but this time I added, "And I know you love me." As soon as I said that, Bill relaxed.

Finally, the nurses told me they could now give Bill more pain relief. They explained they were also going to give him a paralyzing drug, so he wouldn't be moving anymore. It was too dangerous for him to move, especially because his lungs had been burned and the fluid moving within his lungs was causing danger for his other vital organs.

I understood as best I could, but it was horrible knowing that Bill would no longer be able to communicate with me. I'd need to guess what to tell him.

I soon learned that anytime the nurses worked on Bill's bandages, I'd need to leave his room, in order to keep the area sterile. I used this time to talk with the family, who were now in the larger, regular waiting area.

Bill's two brothers, Bob and Scott, had arrived with their wives, along with my brother, Roger. Again, there were a lot of tears and shock, with me trying to explain what had happened.

It seemed forever before the nurses let us know we could come into Bill's room again.

This time the kids and I entered his room. Bill now was lying still, but the nurses continued to remind us to go ahead and talk with Bill, because he should be able to hear us. I went first, since I figured the kids were still trying to get used to how their dad looked. I had warned them about his swollen face, but it was still a shock the first time seeing him. It was hard to look at someone we knew and cared about so much, but hardly being able to recognize him. We then divided the time talking with Bill, everyone getting close to his ear and giving him their message.

Besides numerous reminders of "I love you" and "I know you love me too," I started to explain to Bill where he was, and that the family was here also. I tried to think about what he might be worried about, and what he'd like to know, so I also explained to him the reason he couldn't move, that the nurses had given him a paralyzing drug so that he didn't hurt himself. And I explained that this drug also kept him from opening his eyes. I so wanted him to understand that he wasn't blind, that the doctors and nurses were constantly checking his eyes and they were fine. I also kept reminding him gently of the accident and that his partner had gotten him to the hospital right away. I didn't want him to panic any more than he had to, so I also kept reminding him of the excellent care he was receiving and that he'd be okay.

I also remembered to tell him the family and I were worried, of course, but that we were okay. I explained that everyone was taking care of me. I knew Bill would be worried about me and I wanted him to relax a bit about that. I told him we would get through this and be okay.

As I took a bathroom break, I remembered I needed to call my boss and explain what was going on, since I wouldn't be at work on Friday. She was very understanding, and it took only a short conversation to have her tell me to do what needed to be done. I then quickly returned to Bill's room.

The doctor was now in the unit. He came into Bill's room and explained the severity of Bill's condition. The number-one problem was the burns to his lungs. The doctor explained that if the burns had come from a fire they wouldn't be as bad, because the throat recognizes a foreign object and attempts to close itself. But with a steam burn, the throat only senses it as water, so it doesn't close up, and the lungs get the burns full-force. Because the lungs were no longer able to function normally, fluid would build up in his lungs, creating a very dangerous situation.

I was trying to listen and understand what the doctor was telling us, but listening while experiencing fear, shock, and panic, and trying to concentrate on a subject that wasn't familiar to me, was, to say the least, difficult. But the doctor was very good at slowly and simply explaining the complications of such a burn.

The more I learned, the more worried I became. The doctor and nurses were explaining that the next few days were very important. They didn't hide the fact that Bill could easily die from this. Even if he got past the next few days, there would still be many hills and valleys. This type of injury would be a long struggle. I kept trying to convince myself that Bill was so strong that he'd be able to do it. I decided to only think about the present, and try not to think about the days ahead.

Bill's burns to his lungs were complicating his oxygen levels and heart rhythm. He was hooked up to numerous machines monitoring his breathing, his vitals, and who knew what else.

I was on sensory overload, trying to take in as much as possible. They also had covered Bill with a blown-up heated sheet, explaining that, with such severe burns, the body gets very cold. The sheet was also very light in weight, so as not to put pressure on the burns. His room felt very warm, and the nurses explained the thermostat in his room was in the nineties, also to keep him warm.

They told me the only place he didn't get burned was his feet, because of his steel-toed work boots, and the top of his head, because of the helmet he had been wearing. I was very happy about the top of his head being okay, because that was a sweet reminder about how much Bill enjoyed having me put my hand on top of his head while we were in bed. If he couldn't sleep, he'd ask me to do that. As soon as I did, he'd snuggle up to my hand, relax, and fall asleep. Now, the top of his head would become a constant place I'd put my hand while talking to him. I didn't know whether he could feel it or not, because of the paralyzing drug, but I hoped nonetheless.

The nurses explained to me that they would be changing his bandages twice a day, and this would take hours each time. I wouldn't be allowed into his room during that time. They explained it was time to change his bandages now, so I should go home and try to get some rest, because this was going to be a long haul. I resisted leaving the hospital, but was told there was no room I could rest in, so it was best to go home. Family and friends also insisted I do this, so someone drove me home—I don't even remember who.

The shock had really kicked in for me. Once home, I first took care of the dogs. Then I lay in bed, worrying and noticing just how quiet the house felt. *How can this have happened to the love of my life?* I wondered over and over.

Finally, after many prayers, I was so exhausted that I fell asleep.

Chapter Two

Not Out of the Woods

Day Two: Saturday, June 20, 2009

A couple of hours later I awoke with a startle, and then felt shock after I remembered what had happened. Looking at the clock, I saw it was still early in the morning, but I called the hospital to check on Bill's condition. I got his nurse and she told me Bill wasn't good and that I should get there as soon as possible.

In panic, I called Beth again, who was at my house in minutes. This time when she arrived I was in full panic, crying and knowing he might be near death. Beth and I hugged so hard in the kitchen that we ended up on the floor, my legs not able to hold up my shaking body. But I soon realized, enough of this; we needed to get to the hospital. I cried all the way there. I rushed into the hospital and flew through the routine of getting into Bill's room.

I took my place next to Bill's side, placed my hand on top of his head, and immediately started talking to him.

There was tension in the room. The doctor and the nurses were explaining that his vitals were dangerously low. This was the start of my education, as I slowly began learning what some of the numbers meant on the machines. They pointed out a couple of the very important ones, such as oxygen level and his blood pressure, explaining that if they went below a certain point, it would be fatal.

I was still in a panic as I realized how close he was to that danger point. But I was determined to be strong and I kept talking to Bill.

There was a steady flow of staff members coming and going, taking blood for lab work, checking oxygen levels, checking machines, checking IVs, checking who knows what. I became part of the staff, manning my job of holding Bill's head and talking with him. I felt if he knew I was there, it would help.

Minutes later, his nurse was standing at the foot of the bed, staring at the numbers on the machines, with a surprised look on her face. In panic, I asked her what was wrong. She said it was good news. She told me with a smile that I couldn't leave his side, because when I talked to him, his numbers improved. I was so ecstatic that I told Bill how strong we were together. But he was, of course, not at out of the woods. His condition was so fragile that the day was full of ups and downs—just as the staff had predicted.

The nurses put off changing the bandages in the morning while he was in such danger, but I took a break late in the morning to see who was in the waiting room. I was shocked to see how many people were there. Family, of course, were there and many others.

I felt the tears rolling down my cheeks as I saw just how much Bill and I were loved by so many. A couple of the family members went in to see Bill while I stayed in the waiting area to give them a chance to visit with him, and so I could talk with other visitors. So many people were worried about Bill that I was overwhelmed.

I started thinking about who else we should call and I asked family and friends to help with the calls. I thought about our church. Bill was very active in our small Anglican church, and I needed to let them know so they could start praying for Bill. I was saddened because the rector, Father Sam, had left just days before, going to the Mediterranean area to complete a religious archaeological project.

Father Sam is the most knowledgeable man I have ever met. He also is an archeologist, a college-level teacher, and a man of many languages. I wished he was in town, because Bill and he were strong friends.

Bill was extremely active in the church. He was on the vestry (the church's decision-making group), he was an acolyte (I always found it fun to call him the tallest altar boy I ever saw), and he was always working on countless jobs at church and the rectory, such as repairing pipes, fixing electrical problems, and much more.

I knew Father Sam would be shocked and overwhelmed not to be home with this happening. Just the Sunday before the accident, as Mass was ending; Father Sam had come back up the aisle to stand next to Bill to sing the last song together.

This was echoing a tradition Bill had with me. If Bill was helping to serve Mass, when the last hymn was being sung and the procession was coming down the aisle, Bill would leave the procession and stand next to me to sing the last hymn. With Father Sam standing next to Bill singing that day, Bill looked over at me. I could see tears in his eyes. He was so touched that Father had shared this moment with him.

Father later told me that since he had known he'd be out of town for a while, he just had to stand next to Bill to sing the last hymn.

While Father Sam was gone, Father John was filling in on his duties. So I called Father John and he immediately let the parish know and came to the hospital.

I also called Father Russ, a Catholic priest and personal friend of our family. Father Russ had known us years back, from the veteran's hospital. At the time, Father Russ was head chaplain, and my dad was suffering from heart problems. Dad and Father Russ quickly bonded.

Days later, Dad had a severe stroke. It was quite touch-and-go for some time, but he survived. His life, though, was never the same. From then on, he had to deal with being in a wheelchair most of the time, and the stroke had severely limited his speech. That didn't stop Dad, though. The sparkle was still in his eyes and he loved going to the VA hospital chapel for Sunday Mass with Mom and me. Soon thereafter, I met Bill, and it didn't take him long before he joined our little group.

When it came time for Bill and me to marry, Father Russ was one of two priests who married us. The other priest was the priest from Bill's parish, St. Andrew's. We all created a most memorable, wonderful ceremony.

Father Russ soon arrived at St. Mary's. I wanted Bill blessed as much as possible. I was praying for anything to help. I called a few other family and friends, but most of the calls were made by others. Everyone was being so supportive, but I wasn't surprised. I cried, seeing every new face, and it was already hard for me to repeat what was happening. All I really wanted to do was to be in Bill's room. By the afternoon, the waiting room and hallways were swamped with people coming to see Bill and me.

His friends from the electric company were also showing up, visibly distraught over what had happened. One of them was Pat, the man who had called Bill in to work. He was a very good friend of Bill's. Even though he was younger than Bill, he felt a fatherly protection for him, so he hated the fact that he had been the man on shift who decided who would be called in and where they went.

I tried to remind him that he hadn't done wrong, and that I didn't hold him responsible. Maybe it helped some, but I doubted it. I just kept reminding people to keep praying for Bill.

A couple of Bill's other friends from work also showed up. Cal was back. I could still see the strain of guilt on his face, so I gave him a big hug, trying to remind him it wasn't his fault.

Another friend from work, Mark, had also arrived. Bill and Mark had been friends for so many years. Bill's friends from work were trying to tell me that questions were already being asked at work, and that it would be a good idea for me to get a lawyer. I hadn't even thought that far ahead, so I filed away the thought for now.

In addition to the guys on staff at the electric company, not surprisingly, Bob and Gail showed up quickly. Bob had just retired from the electric company. He had worked many years with Bill. They were so close, on and off the job. Bob and Gail had driven to Milwaukee from the Eagle River area where they now owned a home on a lake up north.

***

Bob and Bill had been close friends for years. I had met Bob when Bill and I were dating. They not only worked together, they played cards together, bowled together, and socialized together. I really enjoyed seeing the friendship between the two of them. Bob and I had picked up a devilish habit of telling funny stories about Bill. It was fun watching Bill's reaction. He was so good natured that most of the time he'd accept our kidding, even when Bob and I were laughing so hard our eyes would turn red.

Bob met Gail a few years later and the four of us really enjoyed evenings together. Bob and I continued our stories about Bill, now in front of Gail. She'd sometimes take Bill's side, saying, "Poor Bill!" and giving him a hug, but Bob and I were merciless, continuing our shenanigans, not only telling new stories, but repeating old stories over and over. I'm not quite sure how much Bill or Gail enjoyed it, but Bob and I would continue laughing until we had our fill.

Now Bob and Gail spent most of the year in their home up north. Bill and I had spent a few weekends with them. And what wonderful weekends! A couple of times, Bill and Bob had gone fishing on Bob's boat. I was fine with that until Bob and Gail started filleting the bucket full of fish. Bill and I were sitting on the stools watching Bob and Gail work, until I realized they were cutting the heads off live fish. It took me a half second to be off that stool and into the living room, pretending I hadn't just seen that. Between the dish of chocolate they always had for me, and my Southern Comfort, I soon recovered, blocking it out of my mind.

Weekends with them were so relaxing. The morning would start with a hot cup of coffee, flavored with Bailey's, while sitting on a chair on their deck overlooking the lake. Life couldn't get more comfortable. We would take walks, sit around having a good chat, and choose what to do to fill the day. Bob and Gail were both great cooks, so we always had our fill and then some.

Bill and I were astonished with the way Bob and Gail got used to life in the North Woods. The last time we were there, they had showed us they had made a pile of broken branches on the edge of their property. In walking around with their dog, they discovered a bear had taken up residence for its winter hibernation. The thought scared Bill and me, but Gail went on to tell how she had crawled partially into the hole, only to be shaken by a bear growling at her. She so calmly told the story.

We asked if they were going to get rid of the branches after the bear left, but she explained, no, she was going to add to it for a bigger nest. Yikes.

***

In addition to Bill's friends from work arriving at the hospital, there were also a couple of the bosses from the electric company. That bothered me, because the last thing I wanted to think about was the company that had let this happen. I didn't want to hear their well wishes, sincere or not. But I went along with it, so as not to cause problems. I didn't know what the future would be, and I didn't want to burn any bridges, just in case.

One more call I wanted to make was to Bill's longtime friend Dave. Dave and his family lived an hour's journey north near Plymouth, in a small town called Cascade. But I knew Dave would want to be here. Dave and his wife Jaci had been church friends with Bill since childhood. When I started dating Bill, they were the first couple I met. We became a foursome from that time on. We also had seen each other's families through other tragedies, including the death of Bill's mom from cancer and a car accident in which Dave and Jaci's older daughter had died. Chrissy was such a beautiful teenager, inside and out. It was a very sad day to hear what had happened.

Now I needed to call Dave for Bill. I got him on the phone and I started crying. I managed to get out enough information for Dave to understand what was happening, and he assured me he'd be at the hospital the next day.

It was now approaching the time of day when the change of bandages needed to occur, especially since the morning bandage change had been cancelled. We made one last trip into Bill's room to say goodnight, and we all left for our homes.

This time, at home, after I took care of the dogs, it started to hit me what all of this could mean. Even if Bill were to survive, he'd be in the hospital for a very long time. Bill was the main paperwork person in our house. It worked for us, because Bill was good at it, and most of our insurance policies were in his name through his company.

I didn't mind Bill doing this because I had a daytime desk job myself, so by the time I came home from work, the last thing I wanted to do was paperwork. But what Bill wasn't, was organized. He seemed to know where to find things in his piles of paperwork, but I sure didn't. We'd had a discussion more than once about the importance of keeping the paperwork organized, in case something would happen and I'd need to find things. We never pictured that this would happen so soon.

So that night, around midnight, I started my new routine of picking up a section of paperwork from Bill's dresser every night, going through each piece and putting them in piles, to decide on later. I didn't know what I'd be facing in the future, but I felt I better get started.

A couple of hours later, exhausted, I fell asleep, making sure I set the alarm. As a night person, rather than a day person, I always had to rely on an alarm.

Day Three: Sunday, June 21, 2009

No alarm needed—I awoke a couple of hours later. I reached for the phone to call the hospital, but hesitated out of fear. The news yesterday morning had scared me so much that I was afraid to hear what was ahead of Bill and me today.

I finally gained the courage to call and was relieved that, even though he wasn't any better, he was at least not worse. I got ready and this time I drove myself to the hospital.

Arriving in Bill's room, I could see his face was slightly less swollen today. I took that as a very positive sign. He looked more like my Bill today.

I resumed my position next to his side with my hand on his head. Holding this position was challenging. First, the room temperature was still set above ninety degrees to keep Bill warm. When you are wearing a gown and gloves, that temperature seems even hotter.

Bill's bed was also set fairly high for all the nurses to be able to do their duties. So to stand right next to Bill with my hand on his head and to be able to talk fairly close to his ear created quite an uncomfortable way to stand for hours. I'd lean slightly forward to get close, but always tried to be sure not to lean on any IVs or press anywhere else on his body. I had to stretch my arm to reach the top of his head. My rule of thumb was, if I felt like complaining, I just had to think what Bill was going through. I'd quickly stop my complaints and just be happy to be near Bill. I'd do anything to stay by his side.

The nurses and doctors were wonderful about letting me stay in his room so much. They seemed very aware of the influence of a loved one's presence on a patient. I tried to stay out of their way as much as possible. I didn't want to make anything worse, nor did I want to give them a reason to ask me to leave.

I had to remind myself to take breaks so that others would be able to see Bill, so I headed to the waiting room. Once again, plenty of people who cared about Bill were arriving at the hospital. Because I was almost always in Bill's room, I wasn't always aware who was in the waiting area. I was hearing that some people had come and gone without me seeing them, especially people from church. They had come to show concern, but didn't want to interrupt what was going on.

Also, so many people were asking the nurses if they could come in to see Bill. A few of the bolder visitors weren't using the phone system to call in to talk with a nurse first; they were coming into the unit and talking with whichever nurse was nearest the door.

Finally Bill's nurse (his nurse varied from day-to-day) came in to tell me that having so many people here to see Bill was creating a problem. She said she'd set up a system so that no one could come in without my permission, excluding priests. That helped, and it kept electric company officials from entering without our consent.

The visitors themselves started a rotation of coming in to see Bill. That worked well, and I was able to see more of the people there. Of course, the kids and Bill's brothers could come and go as they wanted. With everyone so worried, I didn't want to stop any loved ones from seeing Bill.

I also learned that at that morning's Mass at St. Edmund's, news of Bill's accident was announced in church, so a very large prayer chain was going on. People were also taking turns coming to the waiting room, bringing food. Somehow the nurses seemed to be getting their share of the food, and I was glad.

I soon realized what a hard job the nurses had in the burn unit. They worked constantly, and I was amazed how accurately they knew their job. Of course, they were keeping in touch with the doctors, but they knew their stuff.

The family was being so good about calling so many people close to Bill. Some of Bill's cousins were in the waiting room today. One cousin, Cheryl, visited a few times. I remembered meeting Cheryl before we were married. Occasionally Bill and I would take a drive to her house. Cheryl and I had a lot in common, especially our love of gardening. Bill would often complain that we would wander around each of our yards, talking about every single plant. Sometimes Bill would walk with us, but usually he'd give up before we were done and go back to the patio to enjoy a Pepsi, waiting for us to return. We would finally realize how long we had been talking about our plants, and go back and include Bill in our visit.

I tried to spend a few important moments with most of the people that came to visit. I knew how much they were all so concerned about Bill.

As I was about to make another call, I looked up and there stood Dave. I already knew what a great hugger he was, so I was ready. He and I hugged and cried for a long time while Jaci patiently waited. Then I hugged Jaci and we all went into Bill's room so they could see him.

It was hard for me to watch the faces of people when they saw Bill for the first time. I had already gotten use to the sight of Bill's condition, including the multitude of IVs, bandages and ointments used. But seeing it for the first time was hard. Visitors would try to smile and they would talk to Bill, but I knew how rough it was for them.

Dave did a great job talking to Bill, which didn't surprise me. Dave had been a medic in Vietnam, so he had seen a lot. And I was glad to hear Dave talking with Bill. He has a very strong voice and I was sure Bill knew it was Dave.

One of the alarming things to new visitors was the ointment the nurses used on Bill's face and body. Shortly after it was applied, it made his skin look better. But after a short time, fluids would escape from Bill's body and mix with the ointment. It helped when the nurses explained that it aided Bill's burned skin, but again, it was hard to see for the first time.

Bill stayed about the same during the entire day. I continued to believe in his strength, both in mind and body. I was also glad to hear visitors remind me how strong Bill was, and that if anyone could fight this, he could. I needed all and any positive comments to help strengthen myself.

The day passed and it came time to change the evening bandages, so we left for the night. My brother Roger started a nightly vigil of waiting for everyone to leave, and then he'd walk me to my car. He, of course, was worried about Bill, but like many, he was also very worried about me. I understood this, but my concerns were not about myself; they were only for Bill.

I drove home that night, thinking about what had happened over the last couple of days. It was all so hard to believe. I kept telling myself to stay strong and do everything I could to help the situation.

At home, after taking care of the dogs, I again continued my paperwork challenge. I decided if I worked on this a couple of hours every evening, I'd get the hill of paperwork sorted in about a week. But that was only sorting—I then would need to examine these piles.

I also had to deal with Bill's checkbook. We each carried one, with our names on both of them. But that didn't mean I was up to date on his checkbook. I had to make sure his account had enough money in it, since I knew he had some direct withdrawals every month. I had to think about what might need to be done.

I also didn't know how this accident might affect Bill's paycheck. I was guessing I'd need to fill out some claim forms for his time off from work. *If Bill's paycheck stops, then how will I be able to make mortgage payments and pay other bills?* I wondered. I decided to talk with Julie about all of this tomorrow. She was an accountant, so she'd be of great help. Besides, I was too tired. I might make mistakes.

I also suddenly realized that besides Bill being off work, I needed to keep track of my own work. The weekend was over, so I'd need to call my supervisor tonight to explain that I didn't know what to expect. I called her and said that I'd go to the hospital first thing in the morning. When I had to leave during bandage changing, I'd come to work for a few hours. The nurses had my cell phone number, so it would take only about fifteen minutes to get back to St. Mary's if something urgent were to occur.

It struck me strange that since I worked at another hospital, St. Luke's, I'd need to commute between two hospitals. Unfortunately, they were on opposite sides of town from my house.

My supervisor was great. She again told me to do whatever was necessary. That relieved me, to know my job was at least temporarily taken care of.

Ready for bed, my thoughts were, of course, on Bill. He had held on for two days now. Hope was stronger than fear tonight as I told myself Bill was inching toward better ground.

I finally went to bed, trying to prepare for another day.

Chapter Three

The Danger Zone

Day Four: Monday, June 22, 2009

Again, I only slept for a few hours and awoke with a startle. As I was to do every morning, I first called the hospital. Bill had not only stayed about the same during the night, he was a bit better this morning, enough that they were bringing in the rehab staff to move his arms and feet some.

I was happy to hear the good news, but I was nervous about them starting rehab. It seemed too soon. However, they reminded me that, even though he was still very critical, down the line he'd have fewer problems if the therapists could do a little therapy every day. I understood, but was still scared. I didn't want anything to worsen his condition. I quickly got ready and went to the hospital.

Bill's face again seemed slightly better to me. The swelling had decreased a little again, and I thought that Bill looked more himself. His nurse seemed pleased that he had held his own overnight.

The therapist soon joined us. She very carefully lifted his arm and moved it and his fingers a little. I relaxed some, and we started a conversation. But I noticed one of the numbers on his machine was decreasing, which caused me concern, so I started asking questions. I was told the equipment wasn't making good enough contact with Bill's body. They tried to adjust it a few times, but I soon could tell they also were becoming concerned. The therapist quit doing her work and left the room. Blood tests were taken, and the numbers continued to worsen.

They cancelled the morning's bandage change, so I called work to say I wouldn't be in. At this point you couldn't pry me away from Bill's side. The nurses were talking among themselves, and I could tell they were consulting with the doctor. I could see that outside of Bill's room, staff were milling around, talking.

Now I was told Bill was in danger. I vaguely remembered hearing something the first day, stating that the third day was often dangerous. And, unfortunately, it was coming true. The nurses kept telling me to talk with Bill, which I did nonstop. I kept telling him how much I loved him and how strong he was. His numbers still kept worsening.

By now I was recalling anything I could think of. I thought about our wedding day and realized Bill would like to hear me talking about that. I started recreating the entire day, minute by minute. I even did a poor version of singing one of our favorite wedding songs. I knew Bill wouldn't care how I sang; just that I was singing it. He loved the memories of our wedding day as much as I did. Bill had even planned most of the ceremony and Mass. Since he was an acolyte, this came easy for him. I remember being so touched that he had spent so much time making sure everything was just right.

Every year Bill would plan our anniversary. Not just a card—he insisted we plan time together, usually in the Minocqua area in the Northwoods, where we had spent our honeymoon. Even if we couldn't do that, we would both take days off from work, tell our friends and relatives to stay away, and we would spend the time at home. We would always play our wedding tape, watching with our arms around each other, enjoying the recollections of the day. I never could remember talking with a couple that enjoyed their wedding and anniversaries as much as Bill and I did. And I was proud of that.

I knew Bill needed to know I was there, and he needed to think about happier times. But the nurses told me the numbers could only go so low before Bill's organs would be damaged, and those numbers were getting way too close. After hours of work, the nurses told me to call the family to get here as fast as they could. I, of course, knew what that meant, so I called one of the family—I don't remember which one—and told that person to let everyone know as soon as possible.

Within a half hour some of them were already arriving, having the same worried look as I'm sure was on my face.

I also called Father John, and he said he'd quickly come to the hospital. I again was hoping for as many prayers for Bill as possible.

As a non-medical person, I had no clue as to what was being done to help Bill, but there were a lot of staff working very hard. I was trying to stay out of the way, so I stayed glued to the side of his bed as much as I could and kept talking to him. Now, I again was recollecting our honeymoon and some of our anniversary trips to Minocqua.

***

We had been so very broke during our engagement that we hadn't talked about a honeymoon. But one day Bill had lunch with a friend of his, Dan. As Bill told me later, he was talking about the wedding, and Dan asked if he had any honeymoon ideas. Bill said we'd be lucky if we got as far as Cudahy, a nearby industrial suburb of Milwaukee.

Dan had asked if we'd be interested in using his cabin in Winchester, thirty miles northwest of Minocqua. Bill said he'd check with me. He had called me shortly after their lunch. I was thrilled. We laughed, because Bill hadn't asked what type of a cabin it was. We didn't even know if it had inside plumbing. But we didn't care; we were going someplace.

So a couple of days after our wedding, we packed up the car and started what was supposed to be a six-hour drive. I think it took us nine hours. First, we had a very late start—we'd left at about 6:00 p.m. And, of course, we wanted to stop for something to eat. The farther we got in the Northwoods, the more deer we started seeing near the road. So Bill slowed it down quite a bit. We even had to stop once because there was a buck standing right in the middle of the road. Bill beeped his horn a couple of times and it slowly moved to the side.

With the map out, and driving instructions from Dan, we finally made it to Winchester. It was one of the smallest towns I'd ever seen—a couple of houses, a church, a gas station, and a dump. I don't even remember seeing a bar. But we drove up the hill, following Dan's instructions. He said we wouldn't be able to see the house from the street, but they had a carved plaque with their name on it. Thank goodness, we found it. It was next to a small road, which looked more like the driveway of the closest house.

We were married in late October, and being this far up north meant snow. We could barely make out where the road went, but we slowly followed it. I panicked when I saw water just about a foot from my side of the car. Bill checked, and it was the same on his side. We didn't know if we were going to get lost in the woods, or in the bottom of the lake, but we slowly went on.

After passing over a small hill, and then down a slight slope, we finally reached the cabin. And what a cabin! Facing the road it didn't look that impressive, but we soon saw it had a wrap-around deck, and as we continued to look, we realized we were on the tip of a peninsula. What a spot for a honeymoon. We grabbed some of our gear and couldn't wait to see the inside.

It was unbelievable. The kitchen/living room had a vaulted ceiling about ten feet high. Once we put a light on, we were amazed at the view. One wall of the living room had double, sliding-glass doors with windows also above them. It had a great view, but it also was completely private, because of the cabin's location.

The living room also had a potbellied stove with a stack of wood. It couldn't have been better. We moved in for the week and loved it. We cooked a couple of meals, but most evenings we would drive into Minocqua and check out all the restaurants. And what really made it nice was that late October is the quiet season. It was too cold for summer events, it was in between hunting seasons, and it was too warm for skiing and snowmobiles… *it was perfect.*

And what was to come was too wonderful to imagine. Dan's family never went up to their cabin that time of year, so he offered it to us every year for about eight years. It became "our house" for a week every year. We would repay them by doing chores, gathering wood, stacking it, whatever we could do, we were so thankful. Sadly, they eventually had to sell it, but after that we still would go near Minocqua and stay at a motel.

Bill had loved these trips, so I knew he'd enjoy hearing me talk about them. It also did a good job of helping me to not focus on what the nurses were doing.

***

A couple of hours passed and Bill was still in trouble. The whole family looked tired; the worry was evident on their faces. It was hard seeing the kids fearing the worst. Father John had been in Bill's room a couple of times with prayers.

I want to do more, but what? I silently asked myself. I kept talking about happier times, to try to strengthen him. I constantly reminded him that I'd love to crawl in bed with him, but the nurses would be mad about that.

***

Now I started thinking about our more-recent, spring cruise trips.

We had each been campers most of our lives. This was a great way to have an inexpensive vacation. We camped while dating, and continued after we married, including the kids and their friends. We sure had fun on those busy camping trips. But the kids were getting older, and they were losing interest in camping with us. So Bill and I thought maybe we should try something different for the two of us.

One day at my work, some people were discussing how they had been on cruises. Their most popular choice was Princess Cruise Line. I talked with Bill later to see what he thought, and he was interested enough to check it out. Neither of us had done much traveling outside of Wisconsin, and neither of us had ever been outside of the country. But the Caribbean was sounding real good.

So we checked lots of brochures and decided Princess in the Caribbean was it. We were so excited. I had always wanted to be on a ship, but I was scared of getting seasick. However, that wasn't going to stop me. I listened to tips from the people at work, and off we went on our new adventure.

It was better than we ever imagined. We loved every step of every trip, from checking out each area in a new ship, to the endless meals, shows, nightclubs, casinos, and of course, the wonderful places they took us.

As soon as our trip was finished, we would start planning next year's trip.

Our best trip had been a two-week cruise to Hawaii. We loved having two weeks of fun, we loved the ship time, and we loved going to the different islands of Hawaii. We loved this trip so much that we had already booked another one for the following year to celebrate our twenty-fifth anniversary.

***

As I stood next to Bill, I was recreating our last Hawaiian cruise, pretending it was the new cruise coming up next spring.

Finally, as the evening hours were approaching, Bill's numbers were slowly improving. The staff seemed a bit calmer, and very nicely, they told me what a good job I had also done during that day. I felt relieved, but I could see the staff saw this as very serious. I didn't know exactly why, and I didn't really want to find out just then.

I decided it was time for a bathroom break, so I left Bill's room. A woman approached me, telling me she'd like a moment to talk with me. She explained she was a psychologist working on the floor, and her job was to help patients and their families. I agreed, so we went into her office, which was just around the corner from the burn unit.

I sat with her and found out she had already been following Bill's case. She explained how she liked to let families know she was here to talk to, and as the patient improved, she'd develop a relationship with them. I talked very freely with her and she complimented me on how well I was handling this. I told her that I was a frightened mess in the inside, but I was determined to stay strong to help Bill in any way possible, just as our family was staying strong. She let me know she was here for us and our conversation ended. I then wanted to make a short visit to the waiting room before returning to Bill's room.

I stopped at the bathroom first—my favorite place to have a good cry. As I entered the waiting room, my heart felt full of the love from so many family and friends. They were also worried, of course, but always talking about how strong Bill was and how he could fight this.

I had been in Bill's room for hours. Now I needed to give other people a chance to see him. They knew today had been a dangerous day. Church members were also present. Father John, and Father Sam's mom, Betty, were there. After a short visit in the waiting room, I went back to Bill's room with Father John to say prayers for Bill and our family.

I left his room for a while again, trying to let more people see him. I was being reminded by those in the waiting room to eat, but nothing sounded good to me. Bill's brother Bob, told me to at least have some milk, and he insisted I go to the cafeteria with him. He wanted me to get out of the area for just a bit. And he was right; the milk did taste good.

The last thing on my mind was me. But family and friends were becoming more concerned about me. They knew I wasn't sleeping or eating much, and they were trying to remedy that. People were bringing snacks for us, and some, like Gail and Debbie, were constantly bringing items to eat and drink.

Back in Bill's room, things seemed to have settled down. Bill's numbers were where they had been the day before. I was happy with that, but still very frightened to see how fast things could change. The nurses had warned us on the first day that it would be a rocky road. And today was quite an example of this.

The staff decided they needed to change Bill's bandages now, so that ended our evening and I headed home, back to the dogs and the paperwork.

I continually told myself that when Bill awakened, I'd have things in order, ready to face whatever we were going to have to face.

Chapter Four

Watching and Waiting

Day Five: Tuesday, June 23, 2009

Startled awake again, I called the hospital. Thank God… Bill was holding his own again. I dressed and got to the hospital. It was a quieter morning, and it felt good just to talk to Bill. When it came time for the morning bandage change, this time I left the hospital and headed to work.

I didn't care what was happening at my job, but since I didn't know what was going to happen with Bill, I knew I needed to keep this job secure. When I arrived at work I quickly saw how much work had piled up. Thank goodness I had a separate area for my desk, so I had some privacy. But this was the first time back to work since Bill's accident, so staff quickly surrounded me to see what was happening and whether I was okay. I understood the questioning; I'd probably be doing the same thing. And I knew that they were all wishing me the best.

I worked in a cardiology group as their administrative assistant. I also created their call schedule, so having me gone would quickly be a cause for needing others to maintain my position. I sat near my boss, the administrator of the group, and near the research nurses.

As we talked, one of the nurses told me her boyfriend had been one of the firefighters who had worked on Bill. Unbelievable. She said her boyfriend described Bill as a very brave man, enduring extreme pain. That sure sounded like my Bill. He'd go to extraordinary lengths to do the right thing. I was so glad she shared that story, and I was so proud of Bill. But it caused me to cry quite a bit, realizing even more what he had gone through.

I got as much work done as I could, but it was very hard to concentrate. I called St. Mary's hospital and things were still okay. They were still working on changing his bandages. I had been told this takes hours to complete on someone with full-body burns. So I worked for a while longer, and then headed back to St. Mary's.

Today, the hospital waiting area was quiet. I knew that most of the family and visitors needed to be at work. That was fine. I delighted in the time I could spend with Bill, talking to him. And it was nice that things were quieter, because the nurses had more time to explain further details about the machines and what the numbers meant. I enjoyed asking the same questions day after day to different nurses. It helped me to better comprehend the information. Each nurse was so special. I actually liked having the rotation of nurses, because I felt each one might be watching something important that another might not think of. And it was easier to repeat the same questions to different people.

Since Bill's room was so warm, the nurses would check on me to see if I felt dizzy, and they would bring me water to keep me hydrated. I really appreciated that, because it did get very hot in his room.

Bill's room had one narrow window, with a view of Lake Michigan. It was nice to be able to look out the window occasionally while talking to him. It felt soothing, and reminded me of our cruises.

I again started to recreate our trip to Hawaii. The nurse that day said she was finding the story fun to listen to, and the next time she worked she wanted to hear more about our cruises.

As the day grew later, Father John again came to bless Bill. Father John had a lot on his plate. He wasn't only covering for Father Sam; he also had a full-time job as an engineer in nearby Brookfield. I don't know how he found the time to come to the hospital every day, but I sure appreciated it. And he always had a smile on his face. Such a good man.

Gail and Bob also arrived at the hospital in the afternoon, again bringing items for me to eat and drink, and making conversation with me to help give me strength. What good friends. They also visited with Bill and then left as other visitors arrived. They planned to stay in town for the week, so they would be there every day.

As evening approached, family and friends were again arriving. I let them have more time to visit with Bill, since I had spent most of the day with him.

Thank goodness for a quieter day. I prayed often, hoping as time went on that Bill was regaining strength.

It was again time for evening bandage changing, so we all left for the day. Driving home, I again was thinking about the day, and was getting ready for my daily evening chores.

I was surprised as I entered my kitchen to see a package on the patio table. Susan from next door had made me some food. I called her, explaining how nice that was for her to do that. She was glad to do something. She was already picking up my mail every day and was putting it on the same patio table. It was very nice to have food to go along with it.

I enjoyed the meal, and after a few chores, I went to bed.

Day Six: Wednesday, June 24, 2009

Again, I awoke early and called to check on Bill. Everything was status quo, so I again decided to work a few hours and then go to the hospital after they were done with the morning bandages.

Later, arriving at St. Mary's, I found Dave. He had again driven down from Cascade and I again received one of his famous hugs. I needed that immensely, because I was so missing the constant hugs I always got from Bill.

Together, we went into Bill's room. I know Bill must have been glad to hear Dave's voice again. They were the best of friends. I always enjoyed how relaxed they were with one another.

His nurse today suggested that I bring some pictures with me to put on the bulletin board. She explained that it was helpful because any staff person who entered the room would see these pictures and have something to say to Bill. I liked that idea and decided to collect some pictures that night.

That day's nurse at first seemed quite strict. She was, but in a good way. She was very careful that Bill and I would have our time together. I liked that idea, and I quickly learned to like her.

As the family arrived, we were all glad that Bill was holding his own, and we probably sounded too positive. Bill's nurse took quite a while explaining Bill's condition, and just how dangerous it was. We quickly understood she was willing to take time to explain the situation to us, so the kids and I started asking a lot of questions.

She explained the ups and downs we would be facing, not to scare us, but to get us ready for the tough times. She also reminded us that Bill wasn't just critical—he was very critical. It would take much more time before he'd be out of the woods. And, sadly, she explained that even if Bill were to survive, he'd probably be facing seven-to-nine months in the hospital. Even when discharged, he might always have to have an oxygen machine with him and multiple therapies. It was very scary listening to her, but I knew I needed to know the truth.

That night, driving home, I was very much reliving the nurse's discussion with us. It was very sobering, but she was right to tell us, so we would know what to prepare for.

When I got home, I soon realized that Beth and Susan were going to take turns feeding me. This time Beth had dropped off some food. I really appreciated the good friends I had, and didn't mind having some good food to eat.

Luckily, I remembered to collect some pictures for Bill's room. I went into the basement where we keep the photo albums and picked a few. I tried to show different parts of Bill's life, such as us on the Harley at Beth and Gary's house, us in the middle of a family shot, Bill with his work buddies, Bill with the kids, Bill playing softball. I don't remember the others, but I was ready to fill the bulletin board the next day.

I also had to check my phone answering machine. Every day I had a few well-wishers calling, and I kept notes on all of them. I didn't have time to call them back, because I was arriving home too late, and was unable to call people during the day. I had mentioned this to Julie and quickly, she and Bob, her boyfriend, set up a website with daily updates on Bill's condition. Now we just had to let people know what the Web site was. Once that was completed, it sure saved us a lot of time, and it was helping to better communicate with all those concerned.

Now time for paperwork and sleep.

Day Seven: Thursday, June 25, 2009

Again waking after just a few hours, I checked with the hospital. Thank God, Bill was staying firm, so I went to work for a while. My work diet pretty much now consisted of a few

M&M's in my jar of peanut butter. I figured that was filling and sort of healthy. In the early evening I'd have milk at the hospital to comfort the relatives and friends, and later, whatever meal Susan or Beth had prepared. That was plenty for me.

First thing after arriving at the hospital, I put up my pictures. Anything that could help, I'd do. And they really were a good idea. I quickly noticed staff and friends looking at them, talking about nice memories. That was good for Bill to hear.

Every evening there was a constant stream of family and friends. And that was very much appreciated. I don't know how I would have survived all the stress without all of them around me.

I was happy to report to the group that Bill was still holding his own, and again, well-wishers explained that wasn't a surprise—Bill was a strong guy.

Sadly, around this time, Billy, Bill's son, developed a bad head cold. He came to the waiting room for a couple of days, but it was so important that to keep Bill's room germ-free that Billy decided to stay away and get updates from us. I felt bad he couldn't be with us every day.

Today was time for our family members to have a serious talk about paperwork. The topic of getting a lawyer had already been discussed. We had no idea what the outcome of this might be. Bill might not survive, he might be in the hospital for a long time, or he might have serious injuries that could last his entire life. We didn't know the scenario for any of these outcomes, and we knew we needed to be represented.

Workers from the electric company were already telling us that investigations were occurring… and not just within the company. OSHA was now included, and the state also would be investigating.

I decided to call the lawyer who represented St. Edmund's Church. Not only had I heard good things about him, Bill himself knew him because of the vestry meetings. That made me feel better, so we gave him a call. We decided to meet on Monday at the hospital. That would give me a few more days to go through more paperwork.

I had also brought some of the mail I already was receiving from Bill's work and insurance companies, to give to Julie. I knew Julie would do a better job than I, so I was giving her anything and everything I found important.

As I left for the day, I hurried to get away from the lakefront's events. Summerfest was enjoying their opening day, and the lakefront fireworks would be starting soon. I was trying as hard as possible not to think about what Bill and I normally would have been doing that night. We loved to ride the motorcycle to festivals, and we were used to enjoying a fast and easy trip to see the fireworks. Parking was a cinch, since we were able to pick a spot between cars, and we could leave immediately after the fireworks stopped, to beat the traffic.

It was hard not to envy all the happy faces heading to the lakefront. I didn't want to think about that. I reminded myself that we, someday, would be doing that again.

I arrived home to again find mail and food on the patio table. This was easily going to spoil me.

After taking care of the dogs and eating, I headed back to the usual evening paperwork duties. I was making some headway sorting the piles, and Julie had volunteered to do the next step—making phone calls to our financial advisors and health insurance agents to find out about some of the details I'd need to know. We also had to deal with the electric company to see what they needed for workmen's compensation and disability plans. I was so grateful to have Julie's help. With her accounting experience, I knew she'd be way ahead of me with this type of paperwork.

With that, I went to bed to get ready for another day.

Day Eight: Friday, June 26, 2009

Once again, after only a couple of hours' sleep, I was awake. I knew I was very tired, but I was so wired, worrying so much about Bill. I called the hospital and learned my prayers were again answered. Bill was still holding his own, so I again went to work first. I was also making some headway there, trying to solve any urgent problems before I left. I was only working a few hours a day, but it was keeping my job afloat.

When the hospital was again done with their bandage routine, I left to go see Bill.

As the days progressed, I tried learning a bit more about the oxygen and breathing machines. There were so many parts to this, so I just tried to learn one part a day. An important number to watch was his oxygen level. That number was best if it was above eighty. But it wasn't that simple. If that number started getting higher (which was good), they would start slightly changing gauges on the other breathing monitor machine. One day his oxygen level might be at ninety and I'd be happy, and the next day it would be at seventy-five and I'd be worried, only to hear they had changed the settings on the other machine. They were doing this to try to get Bill to breathe a little on his own, which hadn't happened yet.

I sure was glad I hadn't tried to be a nurse. It was confusing for me, but the nurses were quite schooled in this and gave me great confidence in what they were doing. I knew I'd never understand this completely, but it gave me and the family something to focus on. We didn't always see a doctor every day, but I understood that the nurses were in constant contact.

When Julie arrived, I talked with her about the paperwork and she was glad to help me. I was so grateful. Concentrating on my job was plenty. I don't know how I would've concentrated enough to also complete the paperwork, not to mention how much better Julie was at understanding all the work. Julie said she'd have it ready for Monday's meeting with the lawyer.

Roger consistently stayed late to walk me to my car. I appreciated him being there for the late nights, mostly for myself, but also so other family members could get home earlier. What a comfort it was having him with me.

Beth and Gary and Scott and Debbie also helped by stopping at my house to let the dogs out. The dogs were spending a lot of hours alone, so I was very grateful.

I went to bed a little earlier this evening, hoping to get a little more sleep. This was all so exhausting.

Day Nine: Saturday, June 27, 2009

After the usual early awakening and the call to the hospital, I learned that things were about the same, so I decided to take some time to play with the dogs and try to catch up on more paperwork and housework that needed attention until after Bill's bandages were changed.

When I arrived at the hospital, I found Bill's face looking a bit better again. The swelling had gone down quite a bit, and his skin was improving some. Even though I knew the most dangerous injuries were on the inside, seeing him looking better still gave me such hope.

Julie arrived with Bob. What a place to first meet your stepdaughter's boyfriend. Or worse yet, what a place for Julie's boyfriend to meet her dad. Bob was so very nice. We could tell how much he cared about Julie, and how much he wanted to support her.

As usual, the whole family was there. I knew, of course, just how worried they were. They were a constant support to me.

Later in the day, Bill's cousin Cheryl was in the waiting room again. It was time for bandage changing again, but this time I was going to stay later to see Bill after the changing time was over. Cheryl and Julie suggested we get something to eat at a restaurant across the street from the hospital. It was a nice change of pace, and it gave me more time to talk with Cheryl and Julie. When we finished, the two of them walked me back to the entrance of the hospital and they went home.

By then, Roger had arrived. After visiting Bill for a while, he walked me to my car.

I headed home to my usual chores and went to sleep.

Day Ten: Sunday, June 28, 2009

I awoke with my usual startle and called the hospital. Bill was about the same, so I waited for the bandage change.

I was sorry to skip church, but I didn't want to miss seeing Bill every chance I got. I was perfectly aware that Bill's condition could change at any time, and I wanted to be there.

After Mass, Father John brought me communion, which I greatly appreciated. We then went into Bill's room for prayers to be said for him and our family. Father Russ also came to the hospital today. Double prayers couldn't hurt!

Again, Dave drove down from Cascade. I was happy to see him. After another of his great hugs, releasing tears again, I was ready to see Bill. Dave is a strong person himself, and his strength gave me courage.

There were quite a few visitors on that Sunday afternoon. I just never knew who would show up next. St. Edmund's parishioners had created a system to visit us at the hospital, so that not too many people would come on a given day. Some visitors would only visit us in the waiting room, and others wished to be able to see Bill with me.

People were starting to tell me just how much they appreciated the Web site updates. It was nice for me also, because now I didn't have to repeat myself so much, telling people how Bill was.

Finally it was time again for the bandage change, so we left for the day. Driving home became my private time to analyze each day. I didn't try to think too far ahead; that was too scary. So I'd try to stick to the present.

Arriving home, I did what paperwork I could, and then went to bed. Morning meant Monday... work, the hospital, and then the meeting with the lawyer. It was going to be a long day.

Day Eleven: Monday, June 29, 2009

I was soon awake, wondering how long I could exist on only a couple of hours of sleep a night. But I dropped that thought and called the hospital. Bill's condition was status quo again, thank God, so I went to work while they changed his bandages.

It was such a blessing that I knew my job as well as I did. I could do a great deal of it without much thought. I still, however, kept worrying about whether I was keeping up enough. I was talking with the human resource friend I had at work, and she told me to stop worrying—that if I was only doing a fourth of my job, I was still doing more than most employees. It helped to hear that. I relaxed a bit.

Back at St. Mary's, I began to feel I was living two lives. I was also learning more and more what everyone meant when they said this could take a long time. Every day we saw changes—sometimes better, sometimes worse. But these changes were so slight that they were hard to understand, let alone try to explain them to others.

As late afternoon arrived, Julie and Scott were there to meet the lawyer with me. It didn't take long before I knew he was the right lawyer for us. I felt comfortable talking with him. We asked several questions and he either gave us an answer or said he'd check into it. We also decided to use a third-party negotiating lawyer in case we had grounds for a settlement with the electric company. The lawyer said he worked with a company that does that type of work. He'd call them and we could meet with them tomorrow.

Time for bandages again, so I went home, finding dinner from either Beth or Susan, as usual. I'd eat while opening that day's mail. There was so much of it. Junk mail in the garbage, some mail for me to figure out, and pertinent mail about Bill that I'd bring to Julie at the hospital. She was doing an immensely important job of sorting through all this type of paperwork, helping to call companies and completing forms.

When it was time for bed, I was exhausted again. I became glad for this exhaustion, because it would cause me to fall asleep a little sooner.

Day Twelve: Tuesday, June 30, 2009

I awoke with my typical morning startle. Then I called the hospital. Bill was mostly the same, so I went to work again until the nurses were done with Bill's bandages.

Since Bill was a little more stable that day, the nurses showed me how the beds on the burn unit were filled with water so they could move slightly to the left and to the right. They said this normally would have been used much earlier to help dissipate the fluid in Bill's lungs, but it had been too dangerous. Just the small movements they were making showed it was still dangerous for Bill. When he rocked to his left, his numbers would get worse because of the fluid level. They said they had been trying a few minutes here and there to do this, but had not been too successful so far. I was saddened, because any type of bad news scared me.

As I came out of Bill's room I saw Roger talking with a man who looked vaguely familiar. I approached them and Dr. John introduced himself. He was from St. Edmund's vestry, so he knew Bill. The three of us had a short but nice conversation, and then I was told I could return to Bill's room. Roger later told me that the two of them had had an interesting conversation.

Later in the day, the lawyers came to the hospital and again met with Julie, Scott, and me. This time we were discussing the possibility of third-party negotiations. They explained that this would be a long shot, because workers cannot sue their employers, nor can employers sue their employees. The only way to get a settlement is if they could find work or parts done by a separate third-party company. We would sue them, and then that company would probably sue the electric company.

We all understood this would be unlikely, as the electric company tunnels were more than 100 years old and had been made with electric company parts and equipment. It would be hard to find a third party involved. But they said they would investigate and let us know what they found out.

It was a very difficult meeting for me, because I had to re-create the accident as it had been told to me. It was even more difficult to tell the story in front of people I didn't know. After the meeting ended, I first headed to the bathroom for a good cry, and then I went to Bill's room until bandage-changing time.

Driving home, my head was whirling with thoughts of not just Bill, but of all the paperwork now going on. It was very scary to think of the decisions I might have to make.

Day Thirteen: Wednesday, July 1, 2009

I awoke with the normal startle and called the hospital. No real change, they told me, so I went to work. As soon as the bandages were done, I headed to the hospital.

This date was hard, because my mom had died just two years earlier from Alzheimer's on July 1. I started to remember the years when my mom and dad lived with Bill and me.

***

Bill had decided after just three years of marriage that we should take in my mom and dad. They were having difficulty because my dad was suffering from the results of a stroke and needed a wheelchair or walker to get around. I was amazed that Bill had come up with that idea. I understood just how few husbands would have done that.

Dad died in 1989 from complications with his heart. Mom continued living with us. For quite a while she was fine, but around the age of seventy, she began to get forgetful. At first it seemed just a case of dementia. Helping her was tough, because she didn't want help. She loved being independent, and I think she just wanted to prove she was okay. So very quietly, in the background, I'd help her as much as possible.

I finally took her to a doctor who, after giving her a test, decided she had early Alzheimer's. The Alzheimer's increased slowly. She was forgetting how to do basic things. She'd put objects in places they didn't belong, and then get upset because she thought someone had stolen them. She also was seeing "little people" watching her. It was all very frightening for her, but she still didn't want much help. That's what I hated the most about this disease—that Mom was frightened in her own house.

It kept getting worse. Now she'd forget this was where she lived, and ask to be taken back to her house. She now needed help getting dressed, showering, brushing her teeth, and going to the bathroom. I'd help her with these things daily, but most of the time she'd get very mad at me for helping her when she thought she didn't need help.

The worst was yet to come. First she forgot who Bill was. She was always scared of him. Then, sometimes, she forgot me. She'd give me a look that could kill, saying, "You're not my daughter!" I tried to comfort myself by thinking she somehow knew I was her daughter, but it was hard. She seemed to remember Roger more than me, probably because she didn't see him as often as me, so she was delighted with the surprise visit. He'd give her a big hug, which she liked.

Soon it was also affecting her speech, muscle movements, strength, and eating ability. She went from cut-up food, to diced food, to pureed food, to not even opening her mouth.

Near the end, because of our jobs, we needed to have Mom stay at a hospice during the weekdays. We visited her in the evenings. Roger would bring her home for the weekends. But now she hardly moved. Her body was becoming so stiff. Even the yogurt that we slid into her mouth was most often pushed back out by her tongue.

Eventually, breathing seemed to be difficult. The last few days in the hospice, Roger and I took turns being with Mom. On the last day, it was my turn. In the mid-morning she looked especially weak. I told Roger I'd call him immediately if anything were to start happening. By mid-afternoon I noticed her breathing was getting worse, so I called Roger. There we sat, one of us on each side of the bed, holding her head, kissing her cheek.

Finally I noticed that even though she was still breathing, there was no longer a sound. We knew the end would be soon. We watched her, waiting, waiting. Slower breaths, slower. Then none. We cried, we prayed, we held onto her. A nurse checking on Mom noticed us, and I nodded my head at her. She understood and entered to confirm her passing, and to mark the paperwork. Now Mom and Dad were in heaven together.

***

These memories weighed heavy on me as I entered the hospital. First I had lost Dad, then Mom. Please God, not Bill too.

In the hospital room, my focus once again turned to Bill. I was going to continue being strong for him and resumed my chitchat close to his ear.

Later in the day, of course, family and friends arrived. They all were so wonderful. They all wanted to be with us.

The day faded into night and it was time to return to home. Home was becoming scary to me. It was so quiet without Bill.

Chapter Five

The Unthinkable

Day Fourteen: Thursday, July 2, 2009

Again, I awoke with a startle and called the hospital. Bill's status was about the same, so I went to work. It was so hard to concentrate there. I did as much as I could in that short amount of time. I called the hospital, wanting to be there. They would be done with the bandages soon, so I headed to the hospital.

Even under these conditions, I still enjoyed my quiet time with Bill. I hoped he could hear me talking to him. Every day, I'd try to remember something new to talk about. If I couldn't think of something, I'd just retell a happy story about us, family, or friends—anything to comfort Bill. I'd continue to explain why he was in the hospital, why he couldn't move, and why he couldn't see. I didn't want him lying there, wondering what was happening to him. I wanted him to believe he was getting better and that if he kept strong, he'd return home sooner.

I noticed the nurses also took time to talk with Bill. I was so glad of that because we, of course, weren't always there.

As evening approached, Roger came in with a CD of *REO's Greatest Hits*. Bill and I loved this group and their songs. We had seen them in concert a couple of times at Summerfest and at the

Wisconsin State Fair. A couple of the songs were very special to us, so I played the CD and sang the songs to Bill.

Between songs, I still continued to talk with Bill, reminding him constantly that he was my big, strong guy and that he should keep fighting.

When it was time for evening bandage changes, we left and I headed home, thinking and praying all the way... *Please let Bill get better.*

Day Fifteen: Friday, July 3, 2009

I was beginning to get used to awakening with a startle. Yikes! That seemed creepy. I called the hospital and Bill was about the same, so I went to work. As usual, I waited until Bill's bandage changes were done, and headed to the hospital.

I felt strong this day. Bill was holding his own. That was very good news. I knew how strong Bill was; I was determined he was going to fight this and come through. And now, time again for my endless conversations into Bill's ear.

Today I was thinking of "Keys Day." Bill was typical of some men, not liking Valentine's Day or Sweetest Day. I often heard him say, "No card company is going to tell me when to be romantic." But Bill was romantic.

***

When Bill and I had become engaged in 1984, the plan was for us to live in Bill's apartment until we could buy a house. Even though I was back living at my parent's house to save money, Bill and I were already rearranging and clearing out his apartment for my stuff. It was such a wonderful time. Often, Bill would make something romantic or fun out of something mundane.

On the day after Valentine's Day, I was at work. I received a phone call from the guards in the lobby, telling me I had a package there. Surprised, but still thinking it was probably just some boring work item, I went downstairs to find the guard was holding a bag full of chocolate-covered peanuts—the ones that Sears had made for so many years. There was a card sticking out of the package and I could see it had Bill's handwriting on it, so cheerfully I took it back to my desk.

I opened the card in front of the three other girls I worked with. It was a Valentine's card, but the word "Valentine" was crossed out and the words, *"Happy Keys Day—should be a national holiday"* were written in their place.

I didn't have a clue what that meant, so the other girls and I started enjoying the peanuts. Once the bag was half empty, I noticed the bag was still quite heavy, so I rolled out the nuts to find a complete set of keys on the bottom of the bag. There were keys for the apartment and garage, and special keys for the cars, with key chains denoting what type of car they were.

I was so touched. Bill had created a fun and romantic way to welcome me to his world, including his apartment, garage, and his cars. I cried and called Bill, who was eagerly awaiting my call. I could tell he was so proud of himself because of what he had created.

From that day forward, every year we would celebrate Keys Day, with cards, dinner, and other romantic ideas. We told the story about Keys Day over and over. Sometimes Bill would bring it up to show how romantic he had been, and sometimes I'd bring it up for the same reason. Many a woman was impressed with his thoughtful and individualized idea.

***

By evening there were a lot of visitors at the hospital. I was now playing the REO CD whenever I was in Bill's room. I kept it quiet so Bill could also hear our voices, but I also wanted to keep it on, in case it might quiet his worries.

Julie, who was there every day, came in again with her friend Bob and caught me singing to Bill. Bob liked REO too, and all three of us were singing now. We probably sounded lousy, but it was a bit of a break from the fear we faced every day.

Tomorrow (the Fourth of July), Julie and Bob were going on Bob's parents' sailboat to watch the fireworks. They asked if I'd come along. I thanked them, but told them I wanted to stay by Bill's side. They understood.

As I left for the day, I was again anxious to get away from the neighborhood, with all the people gathering for the July 3 fireworks on the lakefront. We didn't always go to the fireworks these days, but my memories were focusing on the times we had gone, and it was hard to think about such things now.

Day Sixteen: Saturday, July 4, 2009

Up again, with a startle. When I called the hospital, I learned Bill was holding his own, so I waited enough time for the nurses to change his bandages, and after some playtime with the dogs, I headed to the hospital.

Good news today. Bill was digesting the food from the tube feeding. The nurses told me this was so important, because it showed Bill's systems were intact. I was thrilled. We made jokes of making Bill happy by grinding up steak to put into the tube.

I tried to not get my hopes up too much when things were going well, because when things would get worse, I'd panic so easily. I was trying hard to stay cautiously optimistic.

I was glad it was a Saturday. It gave me more time to spend with Bill and to deal with this being the Fourth of July. I tried to ignore the view out of Bill's window today; watching the boats made me jealous, which I wasn't proud of. We'd always had a busy Fourth of July, and the quietness of the room was a startling change.

***

When the kids were smaller, we often would have a large family-and-friend picnic at our house. We both enjoyed having so many people over to enjoy our yard. We would set up different types of games for different age groups. There was always croquet following Bill's parents' picnics at their house. The Kaiserlings were vicious with that game, playing against or for someone who might be loosing or winning the game. It often was more fun to watch than actually play. We'd have water balloons for the kids, sometimes a volleyball net for the teen set, and a lot of food and chairs for everyone. As it got darker, Bill always had a stash of fireworks to impress the kids and worry the adults.

As life transitioned from having young kids to older kids who had other plans, Bill and I started riding our bike, sometimes going to family or friends' houses, or sometimes stopping at a festival to dance with the band. We would last until the fireworks started. Sometimes we would go into a park to watch the fireworks from a blanket, or sometimes we would park the bike farther away to relax by ourselves while watching the fireworks. Today the memories were winding through my head. I was praying we would have more Fourth of Julys to celebrate.

***

It was a quiet day at the hospital. I spent some of it singing my selection of REO songs to Bill. I stayed until the evening bandage change, and then sadly went home.

Day Seventeen: Sunday, July 5, 2009

I awoke with my usual startle and called the hospital. Things were steady, so I headed to the hospital after the bandage changes. I felt bad not getting to church, but I was praying all the time, and Father John was so diligent about getting to the hospital almost every day. That day he again came to the waiting room with communion for me. This was followed in Bill's room by his blessings and prayers for Bill.

In the late afternoon the nurses noticed a large spot of blood under Bill's body. They brought in a specialist, who ordered a test to be done with a very large piece of equipment that couldn't even fit into Bill's room.

Immediately I was worried. *What's wrong?* I wondered. It could be something small, but I was worried about something worse.

Now he wasn't digesting his food as fast as before. Bill still wasn't strong enough to have many tests done, especially the ones that weren't mobile enough to enter his room. He still couldn't be moved. Even the slight movement of his bed caused the fluid in his lungs to interfere with his blood pressure and heart rate.

They were taking blood tests. They had nothing significant to share with us—*but what are they worried about?* I wondered.

Family and friends came. I told them my worries. It was a tense night.

I left in fear that day.

Bill, stay strong.

Day Eighteen: Monday, July 6, 2009

I awoke early and called the hospital, very scared to hear any news. Bill was holding his own, and they would be changing his bandages, so I'd wait a while. It was a holiday from work today because the Fourth of July had been on Saturday. That was good news, because I wanted to get to the hospital a little early.

I arrived at the hospital and upon entering Bill's room, I was delighted to have it explained to me that Bill's numbers were again a little better. The best news was that he was, for the first time since the accident, breathing on his own a little. Any improvement was wonderful, but being told this was especially good. The technician had lowered the numbers slightly on the oxygen machine, trying to continue to make Bill breathe on his own.

I started asking questions as I always did, trying to understand as much as I possibly could. They explained to me that they were turning down part of the machine—the part which had to do with the ratio of how much the machine was doing of Bill's breathing, and how much Bill was breathing on his own. Looking at the nurses' faces, listening to their comments, it seemed to me a very good sign—a small sign, but an important one.

I continued to talk into Bill's ear, telling him how well he was doing. The day had started with hope.

I was still worried, though. It still wasn't being explained to me why he wasn't able to eat as well as before. *And what are the results of that spot of blood from the day before?* I wondered. But I tried to stay optimistic, especially when talking to Bill.

As the day went on, his numbers were worsening a little. Bill himself didn't look as good as he had earlier. The staff also seemed to be more somber than earlier. Test after test was being ordered. Concern was on everyone's face. His numbers were continuing to look bad, so the technician turned the oxygen machine up to fully help Bill breathe again.

Julie and Bob and Beth and Gary had arrived. I updated them on what was happening. Now the doctor was outside the room, quietly talking with the nurses. My worry became fright.

They had explained to me days ago that because of Bill's fragile condition, they were unable to use tests, such as ultrasounds, to see what was going on in his body. When the body is so severely injured, the smaller organs can shut down, or at least slow down, in order for the most important organs, such as the lungs, heart, brain, to have as much of the body's energy as possible.

I again was asking questions. There were more blood tests; more worried looks. Julie and I were staring at each other in fear. Now the nurses were sharing that the blood tests were not looking as good. I understood only part of what they were telling me, but the message was clear—he wasn't doing well, and they were trying to figure out why. They took more blood tests. The oxygen and heart numbers were worse.

It was time to call Scott, Shannon, family, friends, and priests.

The day was blurring into night. People were arriving.

The doctor came into Bill's room to talk with me. He told me they suspected that Bill's small intestine was collapsing. How much, he wasn't sure. If it was just a small portion of the intestine, he might be able to correct it. But if his whole intestine was injured, there would be nothing they could do. The only way to find out would be to operate. The doctor explained that it was highly unlikely that Bill would be able to survive the transfer of his machines to mobile ones to get to the operating room. And they couldn't operate in Bill's room. Too many things were needed that wouldn't fit into the room.

The doctor also explained that the chance of Bill surviving the surgery itself was unlikely. And it was unlikely that the intestine was only injured in a small section. The doctor's face, his tone, his explanations... it was all bad news.

It was time for a decision. Scott, Shannon, Julie, and I gathered at the foot of Bill's bed. I explained to them that I understood it was unlikely Bill could survive any, if not all, of what would need to be done for his survival, but we needed to give him that chance. I knew Bill would go for it. Everyone agreed, and we told the doctor to go ahead.

Within minutes, the operating room staff joined the ICU staff in Bill's room. The staff was literally surrounding his bed. They laid the bed flat and started quickly switching the machines to the mobile ones.

The family and I were all pressed against the walls or standing just outside the room. Nothing felt real. *Wasn't it just this morning that the nurses said he was doing well?* I thought.

Then Bill went into cardiac arrest. His nurse jumped on top of the bed, positioned herself over him, and started chest compressions. We learned that she was the hospital's most experienced nurse.

Bill, please be strong.

Shannon, Julie, and I were pressed as hard as we could to the wall to give the staff enough room to work. We were crying so hard we were losing the strength in our legs. Watching this scene was unbelievable.

After a few minutes we received such a blessing. As best as I could understand, the heart attack was over and they were again racing to change the machines to mobile ones. Some staff had left—I don't know why—maybe to set up the operating room. All I knew was I could now get to Bill's side and hold his head and talk to him. Of course, I started to tell him I loved him and that I knew he loved me. I told him he was going to have an operation and that I'd be waiting in the room for him. I told him to be strong and brave. Over and over, I kept telling him I loved him.

The family was also having their own conversations with Bill. I was glad; he needed to know we were all there for him.

It came time to take Bill into the operating room. We were told to go into a private room until the operation was over. I think there were around ten of us: Julie, Bob, Shannon, Paul, Scott, Debbie, Roger, Terry. Beth, Gary... I'm sorry if I'm forgetting someone.

We had sat in this room for a few minutes when I began to feel something was wrong. *We should be praying,* I thought. I wanted a rosary. One of us asked the staff if they had one. It only took a minute to find one. It had been way too long since I had said a rosary, but I knew where the Our Father's and the Hail Mary's should be, so I started.

We hadn't finished yet, but I wanted to know how the operation was going. Someone went to get a nurse. The nurses didn't know yet. But a minute later, the doctor came into our room. I knew it was too soon. He was looking at the floor instead of us. He explained that the whole small intestine was damaged, so there was nothing they could do. They closed Bill up and put him back in his room. Bill would be dying soon, so he suggested we get in there fast.

After a second of tears we headed to Bill's room. On the way I called Father Russ to tell him what was happening. I could hear him crying on the phone. I hung up and headed in to face my last moments with my husband.

I entered the room that Bill had been in these past eighteen days. He lay still on the bed. I stood next to him, telling him I loved him. I again realized something wasn't right. I asked the nurses if they could move Bill slightly to his left so that I could lie next to him. They immediately moved him over on the bed to give me some room.

Roger and someone else lifted me, laying me next to Bill. They also pressed against me to keep me on the bed, since I didn't have much space. I stared at Bill in shock—I couldn't be losing my husband. I loved him so much.

I started to talk to him again. So many "I love you's" and so many "I know you love me's" I couldn't count. I couldn't think of what to say besides that.

I realized that Bill still had the breathing tube in his mouth so I wouldn't be able to tell when he died. So I put my arm on his chest to feel his heartbeat. I was shocked to notice within a few seconds the pace was slowing. I was going to lose him that fast. I cried and continued to talk with Bill, telling him he was going to heaven, and to please wait for me and pray for me, and that I'd pray for him. The beats were slowing… slowing… and then they stopped.

I was about to do whatever one does when their husband dies… cry, scream, faint… I don't know, because at that moment I was hit in the chest—very hard—with a force that pushed my body back and pushed my head back so much that I was glad I was being held up by the men behind me.

The moment I was hit by this force, I knew it was Bill and the Holy Spirit. There was no doubt. I could feel Bill's spirit inside me, inside my chest, my heart, my soul. And at a moment when I would have been crying harder than ever before, I felt a calmness. I spoke out loud to Bill, saying, "You know me… you know everything about me," because that was the feeling I had—that Bill, together with the Holy Spirit, now knew my every thought, my every action that I had ever taken, and it felt wonderful.

But too soon, the feeling was fading. I think it only lasted a few seconds. Then my crying and screaming began. The staff left me alone with Bill for only a couple minutes, and then they asked the men behind me to lift me up, because they were going to take my Bill.

They wheeled the bed out and I stood there for a moment. My legs couldn't hold me and I was soon on the floor, crying. Shannon and Julie were there to pick me up and take me out of the ICU into the hallway.

But what now? I wondered.

I could see Julie turning to Bob, Shannon turning to Paul, Debbie turning to Scott, Terry turning to Roger... and all I wanted was my husband back.

Chapter Six

Saying Goodbye

Roger and Terry and Scott and Debbie both invited me to stay overnight with them. I said I could never spend another night at my house. I went home with Roger and Terry. I think Beth and Gary were going to feed and let the dogs out. I don't remember, but that seems logical.

We went to Roger's house and sat in his new room, which wasn't quite finished. Bill had started the electrical work, but he was only partially done. It felt right that I was in a space where Bill had done some work. And it was good to be with Roger and Terry.

We sat and talked and cried for a long while. Finally, exhausted, they gave their bedroom to me to sleep in. I sat on the bed and stared at the wall. *What's happening? Where is Bill? What am I going to do now?* I was tortured by these questions, and by the biggest torture, wanting Bill back. I wanted to be back in our house. But I realized I was here tonight, so I slowly fell asleep.

The Day After: Tuesday, July 7, 2009

I was awakened the next morning by a different type of startle. There was no hope now, only grieving. I now had to face this world without my Bill. This was unthinkable.

I went outside with Roger's dogs. Nothing was right; I didn't feel part of this world anymore. I wanted to be where Bill was. I guess I was in shock. I wanted to go home. I wanted to feel Bill.

When Roger and Terry awoke, Roger told me he knew I'd want to go home. I was surprised that he knew this, but he did. He drove me home.

It felt right to be home. At least my dogs were here. Now I never wanted to leave here again. Bill was here, somehow. But I hated the fact that I couldn't see him or feel him.

How can one person feel such pain, yet so much shock at the same time? I wondered. I was glad for the shock, as I didn't think I could survive the pain without it.

Wednesday, July 8, 2009

The kids came to the house. They decided we needed to make Bill's final arrangements. I told them Bill and I both had planned to be buried at Valhalla Cemetery, because Bill's mom was buried there. Also, I'd like the arrangements to be made by the Church and Chapel Funeral Home. They had made the arrangements for my mom and had done a fine job. Soon Shannon, Billy, Julie, Scott, and I were heading to Church and Chapel first, and then to the cemetery, to discuss the arrangements.

I was in deep shock and denial. But that helped. I was able to walk through the motions, but inside I was numb. We all agreed on everything very easily. I was glad for that. I needed the strength of the family to get me through this.

Next, everyone came to our house. I needed to pick out Bill's clothes to wear, and I was dreading that moment. So I thought maybe the more people there, the better.

By the time we got back to our house, Beth and Gary were also there; as well as Debbie, David, and Stephanie.

I told them to get some of the large garbage bags I had. With their help, I had them dispose of the things that needed to be disposed of. I had them take the clothes that Scott, Billy, David, or Roger could wear. And I had Shannon and Julie help pick out what Bill should wear. I wanted to do all of this now because I knew after this, I'd have trouble getting rid of anything. I told Beth that I wanted some of Bill's clothes under my pillows, to keep the smell of Bill near me. She helped me choose some of his clothes and tucked them under the covers so I'd have them in bed with me later.

Roger gave me the CD of REO that I had been playing at the hospital. I asked Scott if he could set up my player to only play "I Can't Fight This Feeling" over and over. He was able to do that for me.

This song was so important to Bill and me, starting back when we were dating. We even had the song played at our wedding reception. I have a picture of us dancing to it. And every time we got to see REO live, such as at Summerfest or the State Fair, they would play this song and it would travel through our memories. Yes, that song made me feel even more that Bill was in the house.

Thursday, July 9, 2009

It was the day of the funeral service. Scott, Shannon, Julie, Billy, and Roger took me to the Church and Chapel Funeral Home to see Bill. He was to have a closed casket, so this would be my last time to see him. I was scared to death. I didn't think I could face this.

Inside the room I cried, looking at Bill. I just couldn't say goodbye. The family finally had to remove me from the room, because they knew I couldn't stop staring at Bill. I didn't want to leave him.

Next was the visitation at St. Edmund's. I stood by Bill's closed casket with a picture nearby of him and me hugging. I loved that photo. It was so close to the way Bill and I often looked, our arms around each other, smiling. In the background, the organist in the church, by coincidence, was playing the song that had been the intro to our wedding.

The visitation started, and the line began. I was shocked at the volume of people attending Bill's service. I don't remember ever seeing this many people at a service before. I was so touched by how many people cared about Bill, me, and our family.

I don't remember, but I was told I was in line at least two hours. It didn't seem that long. I remember a lot of familiar faces, a lot of crying, and a lot of hugging. Bill had so many friends from church, from work, from softball, and from playing cards. Some of my friends and relatives came also, but I was amazed at just how many people cared about Bill. It made me so extra proud of him.

Bill's brother Bob stayed by my side the whole time with a box of tissues. Other friends and family also checked often to see how I was doing and tried to organize the group of people.

The service started late because of the volume of people. But I didn't care. I wanted this day to be all about Bill. Bob walked me to the first row. The pall bearers then brought Bill's casket to the front of the church.

Father John was presiding at the Mass, Father Russ gave a message and prayer, and quite surprising to me, Roger stood up and talked about Bill also. That was so sweet. Father John read a letter written by Susan, my friend from next door; a wonderful letter discussing how much she was going to miss seeing Bill walking around the yard, helping at their house, and splitting wood in front of the "wall of wood," as our family and friends had coined it. The wood was so wide and tall it was like a wall at the back of our yard. Her letter described Bill to a tee.

Father John then read the sermon, but I soon realized it had been written by Father Sam, who still wasn't back from his trip due to some bad weather. It was a wonderful sermon. I especially remember a part when Father Sam compared us to swans. Swans only have one love. When one dies, the other one stays alone, never to again choose a mate. I was so glad that Father Sam understood that about us.

The service was over. The burial wouldn't be until the next day, so we all went home for the night. I felt like I didn't know what was going on. This couldn't be happening. Somehow I had to wake up from this nightmare.

Friday, July 9, 2011

I dreaded the burial so much. We drove to Valhalla Cemetery; our gravesite awaited Bill. Father John and Father Russ spoke prayers that I no longer remember. I just remember their sincerity. Many people were wiping their eyes. I mostly stared at the casket. I couldn't believe I was burying my husband. This couldn't be real.

The prayers were over. We all dropped a carnation into the hole dug for Bill's casket. I told the funeral staff to announce that I was staying until the casket was lowered, but anyone wishing to leave could go back to the church, because there would be a luncheon there.

The lowering of the casket was worse than I had imagined, but I just needed to watch it being done. We hadn't stayed for the lowering of Mom's casket, and that had bothered me. Bill and I had gone back to the cemetery later to make sure everything was okay. So staying here now was right, hard as it was.

Now we returned to church for the luncheon that the church women had arranged. It was done very nicely, and I appreciated how many people stayed for the luncheon. But for me, there was too much talking. It sounded too much like a normal day, but I needed silence.

I was ready to go home. It was time for silence and crying. I didn't want to hold it in any longer.

A group of us headed home, and the twelve or so of us sat outside on the patio. I asked Gary to follow me into the house and downstairs. During our travels, Bill and I had collected shot glasses from many of the places we had been. And Bill had been collecting fine bottles of rum. I asked Gary to pick the best of the collection.

We gathered the glasses and the rum bottle on a tray and went back outside. I asked Gary to fill a shot for each person and they were passed to everyone. There was also one shot filled for Bill. I explained this was a tribute to Bill from his loved ones, and I thanked everyone for all their help during the past few weeks. I also thanked Bob, Julie's boyfriend, who had so graciously joined our family during such a traumatic episode.

We toasted Bill.

Everyone now was heading home, back to their lives. I sat back in a chair, wondering what my life was now. I sat there for hours.

Finally, I went to bed, but I just lay there, staring at the ceiling. How can this have happened to the love of my life—my friend, my lover, my husband?

Friday, July 10, 2009

I awoke after a couple of hours, tears streaming down my face. I didn't want to believe this. It was just too much. *What will I do without Bill?* I asked myself worriedly. I moved to the living room and sat in a big chair with a couple of pictures of Bill and me in my lap. The tears were continuous.

The morning turned into the afternoon. My supervisor called. She had worked it out for me to have the following week off. I was so grateful. I couldn't imagine going back to work, not just the coming week, but at all.

Still crying and not handling anything, I poured a strong drink—very unlike the former me. I couldn't change what was going on, so I'd try to block it out. I couldn't stand all these horrible new memories. I managed to go outside to sit on the patio, my pictures and my drink going with me.

As the work day ended, Roger, Beth, Scott, and Debbie came to see how I was. I couldn't do much except cry. I was starting to realize how much shock I was in, and I was thankful for it. People were trying to talk with me, but I didn't really realize what we were talking about—and I'm sure they were aware of that. So they sat with me and watched me cry. I knew it worried Roger sick; it drove Beth crazy wanting to help; and Scott was trying to help with anything that needed fixing. They all wanted to help, and all I could do was cry.

Saturday, July 11, through Friday, July 16, 2009

All the days and nights were blurring together. My drinks were continuing to stay strong… anything to forget for a while.

Debbie was working part-time, so she started coming over, bringing me food and helping me answer sympathy cards. There were so many cards. I was touched at how many people had thought about Bill and me. It took us all week to answer them. I'd probably still be working on them if it wasn't for Debbie's help.

Julie also was stopping by, helping some with the cards, and, thank goodness, continuing to help with paperwork. I felt like I was just drifting in space, not really concentrating on anything. I turned to my most faithful helpmate—chocolate. I started downing chocolate bar after chocolate bar, washing them down with a glass of wine or beer.

Saturday, July 17, through Sunday, July 18, 2009

I think I cried the entire weekend. I couldn't stand to have a TV or radio playing. All I wanted to hear were my thoughts and memories about Bill. If someone started to talk about something other than Bill, I'd catch myself drifting off into my own thoughts. And all I wanted to look at was the couple of pictures I was constantly holding. I was so glad it was summer, so I could sit outside and cry. It was also good for the dogs to be in the yard, instead of them just watching me cry indoors.

Chapter Seven

Struggling to Cope

Monday, July 19, 2009

I finally had to face returning to work. None of this made any sense to me anymore. The reason I had worked was to afford the nice lifestyle Bill and I had—dinners out, vacations. *None of that is going to happen anymore, so why work?*

Yes, I wanted to keep my house, and yes, I'd need insurance and that type of thing. But even that didn't give me much motivation to go to work. I just wanted to be alone at my house. And I was only sleeping a couple of hours a night, so I was always exhausted.

Luckily I had an office area by myself, so if I was crying, it was unlikely someone would see me. And I had a message button on my phone. If I wasn't ready to talk with someone, I didn't have to answer every call. I could check my messages and call people back when I was more under control.

The drive to work was terrible. I was so tired from the lack of sleep, and I had to watch how I drove, because I was crying so hard. I got myself together in the parking lot and went inside.

It was hard seeing people I knew. I received many tearful hugs, but a lot of quietness also. People didn't know what to say.

I was okay with that, because I didn't know what to say myself. Fortunately, I was used to working alone, and I was able to dig into the mess that had piled up. I told myself this might be good; it gave me something to concentrate on.

But working the whole day was just too much. It seemed that once I got to 2:00 p.m. or so, I'd have such a knot in my stomach that I just couldn't stay at work anymore. I asked my supervisor if I could work six-hour days with no lunch. That would get me out of work at 3:00 in the afternoon. Maybe this would help me deal better with work. My supervisor said okay to my idea, at least for now. The hour-and-a-half difference would be considered vacation time. I didn't need that anymore.

Once I got out of work, I cried the entire way home, thinking about how Bill wouldn't be at home anymore. Usually around this time of day, we'd be starting to talk about what we were going to have for dinner. Now it was just me. And I didn't care about dinner anymore.

I got home. Thank goodness for my two dogs wanting attention. At least there was something at home to make me smile for a while. I changed into comfy clothes, and resumed my seat on the patio with chocolate and wine, crying over pictures of Bill and me again.

Soon Beth stopped over. I'd thought I wanted to be alone, but it was good to see her. She brought a salad, which we shared on the patio. She was determined to get me to talk, to get me to think about something else, but that was still difficult. What a friend, waiting...

When Roger got off work, he showed up next. He'd just sit with me so I knew he was there. He didn't really try to make conversation. I just shut my eyes or stared up at the tall trees in my back yard.

Later, Scott and Debbie arrived to check on me. When Scott was over, it was good if there was a Brewers' game on TV. It was something he could focus on, instead of thinking about what he should say to me.

What caring family and friends I have. These dear people became my evening companions for a long time. I was pretty much still in shock, but I remember them being around. Sometimes I'd talk a little, but mostly I'd just clutch our pictures and cry.

Once everyone left, I tried to fall asleep. The best I could do was sob into my pillow and pray. Midnight, 1:00, 2:00, 3:00 The longer I stayed in bed, the harder I cried. Finally I'd fall asleep, only to awaken a couple of hours later and have to go to work.

Tuesday, July 20, 2009

It would be a shorter day because I had to leave for a meeting with Paul, my lawyer, Julie, and the electric company people, to discuss Bill's compensation package.

I had been dreading the thought of this meeting. First, I knew I didn't want to be anywhere near downtown, and the building was right in the middle of it. That thought alone put a large knot in my stomach. But worse yet was having to go into the electric company office.

Thank goodness Julie was coming. We had been in constant contact the past couple of weeks, discussing the paperwork. I was so grateful she was doing all this work. I could never have done it, or faced it, myself.

The three of us met in the lobby of the electric company's main office, and we headed to the human resource department. I was remembering having gone there at least once with Bill, and this was causing me to be more edgy. I was staring at everything, trying to remember.

The human resource people led us to a small room, where one of the union people also was waiting for us. That room was way too small and way too full for me.

I was trying everything I could do to not lose it. One minute I thought I'd break out crying, the other, I thought I was going to faint. I think the shock was still an aid for me.

Julie led the discussion for us, thank goodness; I sure couldn't. It was discussed that I'd get Bill's workmen's compensation, and they let me know how much money was in the 401Ks. These would need to be transferred to IRAs. They said because of the situation, I could have access to a health plan normally meant for retired employees.

As they talked, I was lost in my memories. I could remember Bill and me sitting downstairs in front of the fire, talking about this policy. He had hoped to retire at age sixty-two, and this medical policy would cover him until he was eligible for Medicare. I had pouted because this policy would only cover Bill. I'd need to continue working, and I wasn't very happy about that.

Back to reality… they were suggesting that if I could get health insurance through my work I should do that, because this was a small policy. Next they were explaining that I'd receive Bill's life insurance policy with the company.

I'm sure a lot more went on in this meeting, but I was only taking in part of what they were saying. I had complete trust in Julie and Paul.

The company men themselves seemed to be nervous throughout this meeting. I'm sure they felt awkward sitting with me. Now they seemed happy that everything was all tied up, neat and tidy. All I could think about was getting out of there and having a drink.

It was horribly ironic. Just a month ago, Bill had received his thirty-year service award for the company. Now, after a short meeting in a small room and a little transfer of funds, it was all over. I wanted to punch my fist through a wall.

After we left the meeting, Julie, Paul, and I stopped in the lobby to discuss a few details. I asked Paul if the third-party negotiators had any report yet. He said they told him they hadn't found anything yet, but he'd check with them. It didn't sound hopeful.

I thanked Julie and Paul. Thank goodness, it was time to head back home.

Friday, July 23, 2009

Like most weeks now, this work week was ending in a complete blur. I preferred it that way. It kept me from thinking and crying in public as much.

But this week, something good happened at work. A technician friend of mine came to visit me at my desk. He was concerned and asked how I was sleeping. I explained I was only getting a couple of hours a night. He started strongly pushing me to see a doctor to get a prescription to help me sleep. He thought it would be best to see a psychiatrist and asked if he could check the hospital's doctors on the hospital website.

Today was a good day for him because there weren't many patients. I told him that would be fine, that I knew I should probably do something about this, but I didn't have the gumption to do it. He went back upstairs to the lab.

Since he had brought it up, I thought I'd take a look at the system myself to see if anyone stood out. One look and I immediately stopped; there were too many doctors listed. I just couldn't do it, so I went back to work.

About a half hour later he called me to say he had gone through the list, and there was one physician that stood out to him as a good candidate. I felt disappointed because he only had one name. I thought he'd have a few to choose from.

He gave me the name, and I was shocked. It was the same man I had met at the hospital, the man from St. Edmund's who had come to visit us; the one who had talked with Roger and me, who had told Roger he was a psychiatrist.

I felt delighted about the choice. This man was on the vestry the same time Bill was, so he had known Bill some. I felt it would be so much easier to see him, but felt I'd better check with someone from church first. I didn't know if this would create a conflict of interest or something like that, and I didn't want to be disappointed.

Saturday, July 24, 2009

St. Edmund's parishioners let me know that they were coming to my house today to help me with yard work. I was so grateful for that. I knew I had ignored the yard since Bill's accident in June. The yard had become a mess and it was too much for me, the way I was feeling.

I've learned that once you become a gardener, the upkeep increases. Weeds were growing everywhere, and my bushes were out of control. The grass needed to be cut and fertilized, and pieces of wood needed to be cut for the fireplace. There was no way I could handle even a part of this.

At least twenty good people came that day, including Beth and Scott. Beth took charge, as usual. We walked around the yard, listing everything I found that needed work. That way, when people asked what they could do, I could tell them to ask Beth.

So much was done that day that I probably didn't even know all of it. They even brought food for the entire group.

As the people were starting to wrap it up, a woman from church stopped me, saying that a member of the church who was a psychiatrist told her that if I asked, he'd be happy to give me an appointment to see him. She mentioned the same name that the technician had given me the day before—the same person I had met at the hospital.

I was amazed. This was more than a coincidence. I asked the woman about any conflict of interest, and she said he was the one who was offering to help, so that shouldn't be a problem. But she said she'd ask him at church the next day and would let me know. That sounded great to me.

Sunday, July 25, 2009

I decided to go to St. Edmund's for church It was my first time to go without Bill, so I was very nervous. I wanted to go, because I felt such a strong tie to Bill there. It had been like his second home.

But going alone was suffocating me. Can I control my emotions long enough to get through the Mass? I wondered.

I went as late as I could, so I wouldn't have to talk with many people. I arrived at church and everyone was so sweet... hugging me, telling me how much they cared. It was very comforting, but it also made me cry. I went into church near the back, where few people sat. I just hoped that prayer would help me. But the tears continued.

Bill and I would always join everyone at the coffee hour after Mass in the Great Hall. I knew I couldn't handle that, so I had decided to leave as soon as Mass was over.

I was almost out the door when the same woman who had given me the name of the psychiatrist came up to me. She said she had called him the night before and he had told her it was fine to see him. He even gave her the phone number of his secretary and left a message that I should call the next day to tell the secretary to fit me in later in the day. Once again, I was shocked, but glad. The things that I had been worried about had simply fallen into my lap.

That day, I also started a new tradition. Right after Mass, I'd visit Bill at the cemetery. I wanted to include him as part of my church visit, and it seemed like the right thing to do. I knew this would really make me fall apart, but I needed to be there at least once a week.

Monday, July 26, 2009

On Monday, I resumed the horrible daily drive to work. I cried so hard while driving that it was hard to stop before going in to work. The first thing I did was call the psychiatrist's office. His secretary set up a time for me to see Dr. John late that afternoon.

This was scary. I had never gone to a psychiatrist before. Not that I didn't have a good reason to go, but it still felt very strange.

I knew I needed help in many ways, but my first priority was that I needed to get some sleep. It had been almost six weeks since I had a regular night's sleep. Mostly I was getting only two to four hours a night. Everyone was telling me it was starting to show on my face, and I was losing a lot of weight. I didn't like eating anymore. I'd try to eat a little if someone brought something over, but if I was by myself, I just skipped it. I was already praying that maybe I could die from not eating, and I was already trying to do it. If I got hungry, I just made another drink.

I was shaking by the time I got to the psychiatrist's office. While waiting, I tried not to think of anything, but the secretary gave me one of those multi-page forms to complete. I didn't want to explain what was wrong with me on paper—husband hurt and died, not sleeping, not eating, drinking, panic attacks. I wasn't ready to share all of that.

The doctor called me into his office and told me not to worry about finishing all those forms; it could be done later.

He asked me a couple of questions, and then he asked one that was a stunner. He asked me how long I had been a widow.

That word. *Did he really call me that?* I thought. Yes, I knew it was true, but I had been avoiding it. And then I quickly realized that's probably why he asked—to see my reaction.

I was afraid of more tough questions, but he quickly eased up and made me feel quite relaxed. He took a lot of history, summing me up as best as one can do in a short session, I guess.

My expectation was that he'd give me a prescription and send me on my way. Wrong. He said he wanted me to come back the following week.

I left, stunned that he hadn't given me a prescription. Wasn't I pretty clear that I hadn't slept for so long a time? Don't I look like a person who is devastatingly tired? What's happened?

I went home and Scott was at our house. I looked at him and asked, "Do I not look like someone who needs sleep?" I explained what had just happened, and that I didn't know how I was going to get through another week of work without sleep.

Scott then called Debbie to pick up an over-the-counter medicine for me to take until the next week. Debbie showed up a while later, not only toting a sleep aid, but also with chocolate. What a brother and sister-in-law.

Tuesday, July 27, 2009

I had trouble sleeping, as usual. The sleeping aid hadn't helped much, but any help was better than none. Back at work, I was so tired, as usual. Thank goodness the shorter work days were helping. Around 2:00 or 3:00 every afternoon I'd get such a knot in my stomach that I was grateful to be able to leave at 3:00. I'd try to hold in the sobbing until I got to my car. But I knew my driving wasn't very good, because I was crying so hard on my way to and from work.

Beth stopped over after work, and I was able to give her a birthday present. Luckily I had bought it long ago.

She talked me into walking with her and the dogs. I knew it was good for the dogs, but it so reminded me about the walks Bill and I would take with them, and Beth knew it. I did know it was good exercise for me, and I hoped it would relax me some.

Wednesday, July 28 through Friday, July 31, 2009

By the end of the month, I still was getting no sleep and had no concentration. Work was really getting hard to handle. It was fortunate I knew my job as well as I did, because I could go through the motions and still do pretty well.

I couldn't wait for the days to be over, but that didn't make sense either, because the evenings were so hard for me also. There didn't seem to be a place that I could find calmness. I just wanted to be with Bill.

Besides seeing my dogs, there was never anything special I was going home to now. But at least I'd be free to cry when I wanted to, which was just about all the time. Having a drink in my hand was becoming routine.

Chapter Eight

A Downward Spiral

Saturday, August 1, 2009

It was the beginning of a new month. Time was moving on without Bill. I was glad for the time alone on weekends, because then I wouldn't have to cover my emotions. But that backfired also. Once alone, of course, all I concentrated on was Bill, and the tears would commence.

I was so tired that I tried taking a nap. Thirty-some minutes later I awoke, totally startled, realizing that Bill wasn't with me. That was a horrible moment, and I decided never to take a nap again. It was better to go to bed earlier, even if I wasn't sleeping. At least I was shortening the day. That's all I could think about. The shorter the day, I hoped and prayed, the faster I'd be in heaven with Bill again.

Sunday, August 2, 2009

I went to St. Edmund's for church again. As hard as it was, I wanted to go, because God was the most important person in my life now. And St. Edmund's was my biggest sacred tie to Bill.

As Mass started, I saw Father Sam coming down the aisle. I hadn't realized he was finally back from his trip. As he got to my row, he made a sharp right turn and headed toward me, astonishing everyone. When he reached me he wrapped me in his arms and the both of us sobbed for quite a while, as the surprised parish watched and waited. It was a passionate moment for all, knowing we were all thinking about Bill.

I so appreciated the acknowledgement from Father Sam. I cried through most of the service, especially at communion, because Bill had often served at Mass, giving me the wine to drink.

I prayed so hard that day. But unfortunately, a lot of my prayers had to do with asking Jesus if I could join Him and Bill in heaven. It became my constant request.

Next, I went to the cemetery. I put my hands on the ground over Bill and sobbed.

Monday, August 3, 2009

Still exhausted, I headed to work again. I kept my eyes straight ahead as much as possible, because every time I saw a building that Bill and I had been in, it disturbed me terribly. Even driving reminded me that Bill and I had been together on those roads.

I didn't care what happened at work anymore. I tried to do a good job, but my heart wasn't in it. Mostly, I didn't care about the money, except to have enough to keep my house and my dogs.

I was so glad today was my day to see the psychiatrist again. It surprised me how anxious I was to have another session. Yes, I was hoping for a medication this week to help me sleep, but I also wanted to talk with him. It already seemed that it was difficult to talk to almost everyone about Bill, so I hoped this would be different.

During the session, this time we talked much more one-on-one. He wanted to know what I was doing, what I was thinking. He wanted to know about my life with Bill. I cried through most of it, but I liked talking to him about Bill. I didn't have to hold back. The harder I cried, the more he'd hand me tissues. What a polite man.

This time, at the end of the session, he gave me a prescription for an antidepressant that he said also worked as a sleep enhancer. He explained that he could help me with the depression, but not the grief. I'd have to work through that with time. He also explained I'd be seeing him once a week, and that he wanted me to call him every day this week to see how the antidepressant was working.

I felt safer. Having someone skilled to watch over me brought me some peace.

That night, I was to take the first dose of the medication. He told me to take one-quarter of a pill. I thought, *That's all?* As I split the pill, I wondered, *How is this going to help me?*

But I did as he said. I took the pill and then headed to the bedroom. By the time I got down the hallway, I bumped into the bedroom doorway; by the time I got to the bed, I quickly set my alarm and then fell onto the bed. Seconds later, I was asleep. I guess he was right.

Tuesday, August 4, 2009

I awoke confused. Wow, it was morning, and I had actually slept. I was amazed but scared, because as I was dressing for work, I still felt dizzy. *Can I drive like this?* I asked myself. I ate something to steady myself, and then headed to my car. I'd need to be very careful on the way to work. I had to control the crying, because I still felt quite dizzy. It continued at work, but I was able to stay at my desk.

As the morning passed, I started to feel more clear-headed, so I called the doctor's office, left a message, and waited for his return call. I expected that he'd be surprised at how much it had affected me and tell me to skip the pill tonight.

Dr. John called me back. I explained what had happened, and he reminded me that I hadn't slept in weeks, so this pill had just pushed me over the edge to let me sleep.

I asked if I was going to be skipping the pill tonight, and he said no, it was important to keep taking the pill. And I should take one-half of it tonight. I was shocked. The night before, one-quarter of the pill had knocked me out. *And the doctor wanted me to take one-half of the pill tonight,* I thought.

I decided to get completely ready for bed before I took the pill this time. I even decided to take the pill in my bathroom, so I could quickly get into bed.

Bedtime came and I followed my plan. I took the pill and lay down. But I didn't immediately fall asleep. What a surprise. I expected to sleep instantly again. I started crying as usual, but soon I was asleep.

Wednesday, August 4, 2009

Wow. I had slept through the night again. This time I didn't feel as dizzy getting ready for work. I was back to crying as I drove to work, but I wasn't as dizzy. I was confused, but I knew I was going to follow the doctor's orders. I worked that morning and left my message for Dr. John again.

In the afternoon, he called back, asking how I had done that night. I explained, and he told me to take three-fourths of a pill tonight. I said okay and followed his orders.

That night was like the previous night. I fell asleep, but not as fast as the night before. I was getting the picture. As I was getting more sleep, the pill was affecting me less. But the doctor had explained the pill was also for depression, so he reminded me it was important I never forget to take it. This time he told me to call him in two days—on Friday—unless I was having problems.

Thursday, August 5, 2009

I got another good night's sleep. I still hated going to work, but at least I felt a little stronger now. I was also doing my work a little faster, but I'd still break down and cry often at work.

Crying followed me through every day. When I'd get home, I'd cry while holding the picture of Bill and me. The bedtime crying was also still continuing. I wanted so much to pray more now, but it seemed the more I prayed, the harder I cried. I was begging God to let me come to heaven to be with Bill, but that would get me very worked up. I was crying so hard that I was beginning to not fall asleep as well.

Friday, August 6, 2009

The alarm woke me up, but I hadn't slept through the night this time. I kept waking up and crying. And the crying was still steady on my way to work. But now I was also feeling quite anxious. I got through my morning of work, and called the doctor's office to leave a message for him. He again waited until after work to call me. He asked me a few questions about how I was doing, and I told him I'd had trouble falling asleep the night before. He told me to take a full tablet tonight, and he'd see me on Monday. He also reminded me that if I had any trouble, to have him paged.

Mid-August, 2009

Every day seemed the same. I had too much time left; I was too young. I just wanted to be with Bill in heaven.

I was still sleeping some, but the crying at night was increasing, so it took a while longer to fall asleep. The doctor kept working on this, adding a couple more prescriptions. I learned he was very careful about increases in medications. I told him I was feeling quite tense during the day, so he added a couple of medications for this also.

My bathroom counter was starting to resemble a drug store, covered with the numerous bottles of prescription drugs. But I trusted him. I knew he gave serious thought before adding or making any changes to my meds. I also understood he was concerned about my constant loss of weight and drinking. I knew that drinking alone could change how a medication would affect me.

Late August, 2009

E-mails were the best communication for me. I could read them alone, and feel I was with someone.

Wanda, a girl I used to work with, was occasionally e-mailing me. She had been a widow for almost eight years and I really wanted to talk with her.

The big difference between her and me was that she had two teenage sons. I knew from working with her that she had dedicated her life to them. But I also knew she terribly missed her husband. I thought it would be good to get together with her sometime, and she also seemed to agree with that. The big problem, though, was for her to find time to visit. A single mom working full-time with two teenage boys didn't have a lot of spare nights. But I knew she was trying to figure out a time when we could get together.

Susan, another girl I had worked with, was also e-mailing me. She had never married, but she recently had suffered the terrible loss of her sister. So she, also, was now living alone. We also talked of plans to get together for lunch, but she lived quite a distance from me, so this, too, was going to take some planning.

Labor Day Weekend:
Friday, September 4, through Monday, September 7, 2009

Most of my family and friends were going to be out of town for this holiday weekend. As I arrived home from work, I couldn't stand the loneliness of my first holiday weekend without Bill. Everyone had plans, and then there was me, sitting in the house, crying. I was tired of trying to keep it together and wanted to strike out at something, although I didn't know what.

I sat on the patio with my glass of wine and our pictures, crying. This just wasn't going to cut it tonight. Up until now, I had avoided the TV, the radio, and above all, music. They all brought back different memories that I just couldn't handle thinking about. I wanted to experience these memories without all the pain. *But how?* I wondered. My thoughts quickly turned to alcohol.

I filled a glass with Southern Comfort and a splash of soda. Bill had liked Southern Comfort, and I wanted to drink what Bill had liked.

I had always been a very light drinker. One shot had always seemed to make the drink too strong. But now I wanted it strong… very strong. One shot, two shots, more. The more I had, maybe the more I'd be able to feel numb. Then I could try reaching for those memories.

I so missed the excitement I shared with Bill. I missed the music we'd listened to and danced to. I missed looking at our photo albums together. I missed the wonderful hugs. I missed everything. *I missed Bill.*

I wanted to feel something of what I was missing. I had been too scared to listen to our songs—like the ones by REO—since Bill's passing, but now I wanted to hear them. I wanted to look at more pictures... all of them... and all of our wedding pictures. I decided I could only do this drunk.

So I drank more, turned the volume up on my REO CD, and drank more again. Now I was bawling, singing, and drinking... great combination. I was gathering pictures I wanted to look at. The wedding album quickly was becoming a favorite, but not for the standard photos, in which we were looking into the camera. I wanted the photos that showed Bill and me looking at each other, dancing with each other, touching each other. I wanted to look at what I didn't have any longer. I wanted to remember every detail about our wedding day. I wanted to feel the pleasure of it.

The evening, and then the weekend, became a blur. I kept up the drinking, listening to the songs and looking at the photos all weekend. I sat in one chair for hours. And I had no thought of food. Food meant I'd continue to survive this nightmare; I didn't want that. I wanted to be where Bill was.

I knew the chance of anyone coming over was slight, so I wasn't worried about that. I wanted to feel as close to Bill as possible. As hard as it was, it was better than accepting being alone. I wanted to grab hold of what Bill and I had had.

I kept this up for four days. Sick as I felt, I wanted to feel the raw emotions. They were better than reality.

Tuesday, September 8, 2009

Getting up Tuesday morning for work was so rough. I felt terrible after my weekend binge. And I felt very depressed that things were back to the horrible routine that I had been dealt.

I drove to work crying, just like always. I quietly did my work, waiting for this workday to be over.

That day I had my appointment with Dr. John, so I began focusing on that. I knew it was going to be tough, telling him about my weekend binge, and the skipping of any food. I understood that I was making it more difficult for him to work on my medications when I wasn't taking care of myself. And I was losing more weight than I had realized. Yes, friends and relatives had been telling me I was too skinny, but when a doctor says it, it's a different story.

At the appointment, Dr. John told me about the importance of holding down the drinking and eating more sensibly. But I was thinking about what the weekend had shown me—if I was careless about my health maybe that would bring me to Bill.

Maybe this would be the solution.

I went home that night and drank again, looking at my pictures and listening to REO.

Wednesday, September 9, 2009

The days were continuing to be a blur. I waited for the workday to be done, so I could get home and continue my drunken music sessions. Many messages were on the answering machine, because I was too drunk and the music was too loud for me to hear the phone. I also think Roger, Scott, and Beth were still stopping by, but I didn't even know it. I'd find food in my refrigerator from Beth and on the patio from Susan next door. Beth was starting to get angry about how I wasn't taking care of myself.

Thursday, September 10, 2009

I got another e-mail from Wanda. She was going to come over tonight for a visit, and I was looking forward to it.

She brought some brochures from some of the grief sessions she had attended. It surprised me to find out that she was still attending these, since it had been eight years since her husband had died. It had me thinking maybe I should try one of these sessions.

As we talked, Wanda told me how she took pride in carving out a new life for herself and her two boys. I understood that, but listening to her made me realize how different our situations were. I didn't feel like carving out a new life, and I didn't know if I'd ever feel differently. She explained I needed to give it time, but I just didn't believe that.

Wanda was shocked by my loss of weight. I hadn't realized it was that noticeable. We also discussed the drinking. I explained I drank to block out the feelings I was having—not a good excuse, but an accurate one.

If I had thought clearly about it, I would've realized how much my friends and my relatives would be noticing how much I was now drinking and how thin I had become. But I wasn't thinking clearly about anything. I was just thinking about getting closer to Bill.

Friday, September 11, 2009

I'd had enough of the week. Once home, I started drinking heavily again. I wanted to be outside on the swing that Bill and I often sat on, but I also wanted to hear REO very loudly. I tried playing an album on a phonograph, so I could hear the music better. It took many trips back and forth before I had it right. By the time I had everything in place though, I was severely drunk and was lying on the swing, now half-asleep. Debbie showed up. I knew it was her, but I was too drunk to say anything.

She patted my hand and left. I felt terrible knowing how bad she must have felt, seeing me this way. Shortly after, Roger showed up. I saw him sitting on the patio, but he was leaving me alone, letting me do my thing. I knew he wanted to be here in case I needed him. I passed out again, and when I finally awoke, I now saw Scott was here. I felt so bad making everyone so concerned, but my thoughts still were only for Bill.

As I woke more, I started to feel pretty sick to my stomach, so I was done drinking for the night. Scott was watching the Brewers on TV, so I went and sat with him for a while. I told Scott he should leave, that he had a family himself to take care of. Scott reminded me that he missed Bill also, and that being here helped him feel close to Bill. I never asked him again to leave.

It was a wonderful moment, being told by someone else that they were also missing Bill so much. I loved how they were all caring for me, but I was so sad that I couldn't reciprocate. I could only think of Bill.

Saturday, September 12, 2009

Beth had started a routine of us getting together on Saturday mornings. I appreciated her efforts as she tried to find things I might enjoy. Most of the time we went rummaging. A lot of the time I was just following her around, but it was good to get out. And we always got something to eat. Beth was determined to get me to eat.

Back home alone in the afternoons; I'd start my heavy drinking again. I had found my way of trying to cope. It wasn't a good way, but I did it anyway. Soon I had the music blaring again while, through tearful eyes, I looked at numerous pictures of Bill.

As the evening progressed, I drank faster and faster. I could feel the room circling in my head. I felt such a desperate need to be with Bill. I started thinking up ways to get to him.

I knew I was out of control. And I was worried that I'd do something that would send me straight to hell. I needed help.

I called the psychiatric hospital to page Dr. John. He called me back quickly, asking what was going on. I explained I was out of control and I wanted to be with Bill. I'm sure he quickly understood just how drunk I was. He also had to be able to hear the loud music in the background. He asked if I wanted to come to the hospital. I wasn't sure at the time if he was really asking me, or if he was telling me that is what was going to happen. I told him I'd stop drinking for the night, and he explained if I needed any further help I should call him back.

Mid-September, 2009

Days of drinking—and not eating—continued. I was amazed that I was actually getting my work done during the day. I knew I was annoying everyone, but that didn't matter to me. My priority was to somehow be with Bill, so I continued. I did a lot of praying, hoping that Bill was in heaven. I realized how important prayer was. I had always considered myself a pretty good Catholic, but the intensity of my faith now had taken on a whole new meaning. I needed to talk with Jesus and ask him to take care of Bill, and ask him if I could also go to heaven soon.

I knew I was living two lives... the faithful Christian, praying all the time, and the widow who wanted nothing else but to get to Bill—if not by God's will, then by my own will. I knew this was wrong, but I couldn't stop it. I thought about it all the time. And I asked for Jesus' forgiveness all the time.

People were also very nicely giving me books to read. Some were about being a widow, and some were religious topics. It helped a bit to fill at least some of my evenings with reading. I was also starting to read the Bible. I was still drinking, but at least reading helped a little to slow down the sorrow I was feeling.

Late September, 2009

I told Dr. John about a movie I had watched years ago called *The Ghost and Mrs. Muir.* He had never seen it, so I explained it to him. There was a woman that moved into a seashore house that was haunted by the sea captain who used to own it. The movie hinted at the love that was evolving between the two of them. But the woman was worried about what the future held, because she couldn't be with him. He decided to let her think it was all a dream for now. So she lived her life by herself in the house and on the seashore, daydreaming about him. She finally died at the end of the movie, and the ghost was there in a second, holding her hand as they walked off together. That's how I saw Bill and me—I was waiting for when I could be with him again. Like Mrs. Muir, I didn't feel a part of this world. I was just waiting for the next, more important reality, and I prayed that God would allow me to go to heaven where He and Bill were.

Early October, 2009

It continually helped that some of my friends and relatives were occasionally e-mailing me. It kept me in touch with at least some people.

My friend Susan was e-mailing me often. Even though we didn't work together anymore, we had built up a lasting friendship. She had a way of taking even the bad parts of life and coping with them through humor. She liked to tease me about seeing a psychiatrist, always taking his side, saying she was sorry for him having to deal with me. But in the end, she'd compliment me on how I was at least trying to do something about the situation.

I always knew she was teasing me, and it would cause me to smile at my computer when hardly anything else ever caused me to smile.

Monday, October 26, 2009

It was our twenty-fourth anniversary. This was the hardest day yet. I told family and friends not to come over that night; I wanted to be alone.

I first had my appointment with Dr. John after work. He knew how difficult this night was going to be for me. I found some comfort in knowing he understood this.

I left to go home, anticipating a horrible evening. It was as hard as I had imagined. I bought a bottle of the same Zonin champagne that we'd had at our reception, but this time, I drank the whole bottle from our wedding glasses by myself... sad. Then I watched the video of our wedding Mass. It was indescribably difficult to watch, but it was what I wanted to see. I sobbed the whole evening.

At bedtime I started looking at and reading some of the greeting cards Bill had given me. The last anniversary card, from October 26, 2008, Bill had written:

> ... *after meeting twenty-six years ago on 5-28-82, at Johnny's (where we met), Love, From Honey.*

I very much realized just what a blessed person I was to have had a husband like Bill. Very few people have experienced the joy we received from our marriage.

Now it was time to try to sleep. It took quite a while.

Chapter Nine

Changing Seasons

Saturday, October 31, 2009

As the weather turned colder, the leaves were dropping in the yard. Raking leaves was something that Bill, Mom, and I had done every year. It usually took us several days to complete the job. Our huge maple trees are beautiful, but they drop large leaves that don't deteriorate fast.

Usually Bill would use the lawn mower to blow the leaves toward the street. Then Mom and I would push the large piles into the street. After Mom died, Bill and I missed her help. Now with Bill gone, I didn't know what to do. I knew I couldn't manage it all by myself.

Then my in-laws came to help. Bob, who was now Julie's fiancé, owned some large leaf blowers, so Julie donned her "leaf outfit" and started on one end of the yard. Billy used another blower on another end. Scott, Debbie, Stephanie, and I used the rakes, and David climbed up onto the roof to empty the gutters.

After a couple of hours of hard work, we were done. I knew I'd have more clean-up in a week or so, but the majority of the leaves were gone and I was very appreciative.

Early November, 2009

As the temperature continued to drop, decisions about my fireplace became urgent. The existing fireplace had many firebricks coming loose. It would be costly to redo the box, and it wasn't very efficient at blowing the heat into the room.

I found a fireplace booklet that Billy had given Bill. I paged through this booklet, wondering what kind Bill had been thinking about. I chose one that I thought might be it. I was right—on the back page, Bill had written down all the pertinent information about this unit. Wow... we had both picked the same one.

I decided to go ahead with this unit, and it was installed very quickly.

It was also time to fill up the wood bin. Billy, Scott, David, and Stephanie all helped me with this painful job.

Monday, November 2, 2009

Going to work was becoming more and more difficult. A lot of changes were happening there, and this was making it even harder to just do my work and be alone. I still didn't want to talk or hear conversations from other people. It reminded me of the old life I had led, not the new life I was dealing with now. I knew I had to do something.

I sat near the human resources person in our department. She was very comforting about what had happened to me, and we became close friends. I could ask her any questions I had about my benefits, and she'd help me. I found out from her that I might be eligible for disability payments through work. It would be a long process, but it was worth a try.

I also started checking the Aurora website to see if there were any programs for the loss of a spouse. I found a weekly evening group that was starting soon, so I decided to sign up. I checked with Dr. John first to see if this was okay. He said it would be fine, if that's what I wanted to do.

Tuesday, November 3, 2009

I was so nervous about the first day of the grief support group. I walked in and wasn't comfortable with how small the room was. Everyone was tightly seated at a long table. It felt way too close for me.

The meeting started with introductions from the leader of the group. She explained her own situation in which, years back, she had lost her husband. She had become a group leader, and a few years later, a widower came to one of her groups. They were attracted to each other and decided to marry. This man was also part of our group.

This was definitely not the kind of story I wanted to hear at my grief session—that a married couple was going to lead the group.

The next step was also hard. We went around the table introducing ourselves, and explaining our story. I wasn't ready to explain to strangers what I had just gone through, nor did I want to hear all their stories. But there was no choice; my turn was coming closer by the minute. I cried through my explanation. By the time the session was over I knew I didn't like it. I probably should have quit right then. But I thought I'd talk with Dr. John first.

Monday, November 9, 2009

At my next appointment with Dr. John, I explained how much I didn't like the group. He reminded me that I could quit going at any time. I explained that I had decided to try one more week, just in case it would improve. He listened and said that would be fine.

Tuesday, November 10, 2009

At the next group session, there was way too much chit-chat for me, and not enough talk about the important things, as far as I was concerned. I didn't like the session, but it wasn't as bad as the previous week, so I decided to try one more.

Tuesday, November 17, 2009

At the third session, my decision was quickly reached. The leader of the group started happily talking about how she and her husband had celebrated their anniversary during the past week, and how they had gone out to dinner. I thought, *What is wrong with her? Why does she think we want to hear about her anniversary?* I watched the faces of the group participants. Some of them seemed interested. These were nice people, but I definitely wasn't in the right group. I didn't match these people at all. I just wanted the session to be over.

Wednesday, November 18, 2009

The next day I wrote a letter to the group leader to explain I wasn't coming back to the group, that it wasn't right for me.

I was sad that the group wasn't a help to me, but I felt relieved that I wasn't going back. I knew they weren't going to be talking about the things that were happening in my life now, and those were the things I wanted to talk about. I discussed all this with Dr. John. He agreed that I shouldn't participate in something that wasn't helpful for me.

Thursday, November 19, 2009

As I found work getting harder to handle each day, I was still thinking about going on disability. I had explained my thoughts to Dr. John and he said he'd back me up and fill out whatever forms I needed to complete. He was worried, though, that if I stopped working, I might not do anything or see anybody, and that would be bad.

The human resource person at my work gave me the name and phone number of the person I should talk with. It was explained to me that first I'd be out on leave for a set amount of days. When that was done, I'd apply for disability.

Saturday, November 21, 2009

It was my birthday—not a day I wanted to think about. The thought of celebrating anything, especially a birthday, seemed so outrageous. But my relatives, including Beth and Gary, were so sweet. They showed up to make sure I was okay. It was quite a bittersweet day, but having them around helped me.

Wednesday, November 25, 2009

It was the day before Thanksgiving. My work decision was made. After much thought, I gathered what few personal things I had at work and left for the day, knowing I'd never return. I said nothing to anybody. I knew the human resource people would take care of that.

I cried the whole way home and drank a lot that evening. I was having the whole family over for dinner the next day, so I still needed to make the pies. This wasn't an easy task, with the amount of drinking I had done. Finally finished with preparations done, I cried myself to sleep.

Thursday, November 26, 2009

On Thanksgiving Day I was up early, by myself, to get the turkey and stuffing ready to put in the oven. For years, Mom and I always had put the turkey in the oven. After Mom died, Bill would get up with me so I wouldn't have to do it by myself. But now I was alone.

I was very unsure how I was going to handle this day, especially since it was the first Thanksgiving without Bill. And I didn't know how hard this would be on the in-laws. They were also missing a father and a brother. Our house had always been the holiday house, and I'd cook up a large meal, Kaiserling style. I was glad the family wanted to celebrate at our house, but I was concerned about whether I could pull it off. *Will I be able to make—and eat—one of our traditional meals, while constantly thinking that Bill should be here?* I was so skinny. I hardly ate. And I'd get so tired.

Sitting down after the blessing and toasting, I put just a bit of food on my plate. Scott was sitting next to me, and I had to get up for something. When I came back, there was another piece of turkey on my plate. Sweet Scott... trying to feed me.

It was good to have the family all together, but very difficult to not see Bill at the head of the table.

Early December, 2009

It definitely felt better being home than going to work. Gone were the crying fits driving to and from work. And when I felt like crying, I could, without having to hold it in. And it was nice being with my dogs more. They could calm me down better than most other things.

But Dr. John was right. I'd have to watch my tendency to isolate. I was getting very depressed, not talking with anyone.

Luckily for me, Beth didn't allow this on Saturday mornings—she continued to get me out of the house for shopping or walking the dogs. It was good she was doing this, but it was hard fighting my inclination to stay at home. And I was very picky where we went. I didn't want to be any place that Bill and I had been. Even driving past some places upset me. Beth tried so hard, but it was beginning to get to her also.

The approaching winter was also a worry to me. Bill had always taken care of most of the plowing and shoveling around the house.

Mid-December, 2009

I found out that St. Edmund's held a Bible study on Wednesday mornings. I had never been to one before, but I thought it would be a good place to go. Finally, I had a chance to be part of a group talking about God and heaven. I jumped at the chance.

After just one session, I was sold. Father Sam was teaching the Bible from Page One forward—terrific! I already was reading the Bible at home, so this would be perfect. And Father Sam was an amazing teacher. Since he had such a varied background, including his archeology work, he made the sessions so interesting. It was like being in the Holy Land in person. I knew I'd be attending every Wednesday.

Billy soon came over to show me how to use the snow blower. Yuck. I couldn't believe I'd be using this. I remember the day Bill got the snow blower from Sears. I came home from work and he was trying it out. I saw just how big it was and told him, "If you like it, then it's fine. But I'm never going to use it."

Now I was getting lessons on how to start and use it. I had to get out a tablet and pen. I knew I'd never remember the instructions.

Of course, we had a lot of snow that winter. So here I was, dressed in layers of clothing, trying to maneuver this large machine. During my first attempt, I was exhausted after just a short time. Thank goodness Susan called out from next door, telling me this snow was especially wet, so don't worry—it wasn't always this bad. She must have been watching me struggle.

I also had a lot of paperwork to do. The human resource people explained that the disability insurance was controlled by a company they contracted with. And it was common to be denied after the first attempt. They were correct—I was denied, and I had to complete a huge second set of papers. Dr. John also had to do the same. He was so helpful with the paperwork. Now it was time to wait and wait and wait for their response.

My drinking continued.

Late December, 2009

Now it was time to face Christmas. How I wished I could skip the whole thing. Thankfully, the family still wanted Christmas Eve at our house. That would help.

Beth had taken me shopping to get Christmas gifts for everyone, so that was covered. When Beth's family had gone out to get their Christmas tree, they also got one for me. I was very thankful for that.

Getting the Christmas tree had been a huge tradition for Bill, me, and the family. We would always go on the Saturday after Thanksgiving. We would load up the car with Mom, the kids, the trailer, and Bill's chain saw, and head out to one of those lots where people can cut down their own tree. Bill loved having his chain saw, because he could walk around and help other people cut their trees down also.

The group grew as Scott's family would come in their car, and Beth's family would also join us in their car. We would deliver the trees to both Scott's and Beth's houses, and then everyone would come back to our house to help set up our large tree. We have a cathedral ceiling in the living room, so Bill loved having a tall tree.

Afterward, we would reheat the leftovers from Thanksgiving, and we would all enjoy a huge meal and drinks to go with it. It was the beginning of the Christmas season for us, and we loved it.

Now I couldn't even imagine having a tree in my house. I asked Beth to get a small one for me. They did pretty well, and helped me put it up. It was very difficult seeing it there.

I couldn't imagine putting up all the decorations. I had always loved Christmas decorations, and delighted in putting them everywhere in the house. I had gotten so many of them during the many trips rummaging with Beth, but now I didn't want all that celebration around my house. I wanted the religious decorations and the ornaments that meant something personal—ones that my parents had, or special ones I had bought for Bill and me. I had way too many of the sillier decorations now, and wanted them out of my house.

I came up with a wonderful idea. I called four nursing homes and asked them if they could use decorations for either their lobby area or people's rooms. They were very glad to accept this. So I went through all my decorations and loaded two containers for each nursing home.

Delivering them was very special. I brought them into the lobby and the people all seemed excited to accept my gifts. At least something good was coming out of this.

I decorated our house with what was left. I didn't put everything up—it was too hard. But I did what I had to do.

December 24, 2009

Waking up Christmas Eve morning came with a startle. *How am I going to get through this?* I wondered. The family was coming for dinner and opening presents. I hadn't cooked since Thanksgiving, so I was wondering if I was going to remember what needed to be done. But luckily, everyone seemed to enjoy the ham dinner. And opening the presents went quickly, so that was good. It was hard on me, but I also had to remember it was hard on the rest of the family. And having them all here was so nice.

I think the hardest part of the day was after everyone had left. I used to finish cleaning up the kitchen while Bill picked out some of the cassettes he had recorded with Christmas music. I'd join him downstairs to snuggle on the couch with the fireplace crackling, and we'd listen to the music. It had been the perfect way to finish the night. Now I finished cleaning the kitchen as fast as I could, took the dogs out, and went to bed to think about Bill.

December 25, 2009

I decided to join Scott's family at their church, St. Peter's, for Christmas Day Mass. Debbie and I talked about how the music was going to be tough to hear, and we were right. Tears came down our cheeks, and sweet David and Stephanie snuggled with us. Afterward, I went to the cemetery for an even harder cry.

Chapter Ten

New Year, Old Heartaches

January 2010

The cold weather meant I wanted to stay in the house even more than before. I understood why Dr. John was concerned about me isolating myself, but I felt more comfortable wallowing at home in my grief and depression, without having to offer explanations to anyone.

I was still playing the same REO song, "I Can't Fight This Feeling," all day and all night long. Somehow it felt right, as if Bill was closer to me somehow.

Scott and his family were coming about once a week, usually bringing something to eat and giving me some company. Scott and the kids would snow blow and shovel for me, and they would help load some of the wood into my basement to keep my fireplace going. Billy had dropped off a huge load of wood earlier in the fall, so it was great getting help stacking some of it and using our chute to put some in the basement wood bin for burning later.

Scott would check around the house and in the garage to see if anything wasn't working. He'd also check the fluids in my cars. I so appreciated this, because it was something I hadn't had to do for years. Bill had always taken care of these things.

The kids would also bring a DVD of one of the latest animated movies. Those were pretty easy to watch, so I enjoyed the time with them. I looked forward to their visits and the hugs from the kids.

Once again, I called to check on the status of the disability payments. No word yet.

I kept on drinking and was still having trouble sleeping.

February 2010

Beth was still coming over on Saturday mornings. It was too cold to walk the dogs, so she asked me what else we could do. I knew I wanted to sort through Bill's coins that he had collected. He had so many of them, but I didn't want to do it alone, so I asked Beth and she immediately said yes, she'd help. Beth was more comfortable with something to do, rather than just sitting and talking. She knew I was having trouble talking about everything, so it was easier to talk when we were also doing something else.

Later, we would often go someplace for lunch. I loved that. Beth quickly learned that I always wanted to eat at a Mexican restaurant. That worked, because she also loved Mexican. But the real reason was that I was having difficulty eating the type of food Bill liked. And I'd not go to a restaurant that Bill and I had eaten in. I didn't even want to eat at a place with the type of food Bill would like.

It didn't make much sense, but I think it had to do with trying not to relive what Bill and I had previously done. The comparison between then and now was very strong. I wasn't able to think about past memories with Bill. My thoughts were of the future—getting to where Bill was now.

Beth was trying to get me to keep in touch with some of my past friends. I told Beth that I hadn't heard from most of them for a long time, but she shoved it right back to me, saying they were probably worried about disturbing me. She wanted me to make an attempt at calling them. Easier said than done for me right now.

I told Beth I was still getting e-mails from Wanda and Susan, and that I'd suggest getting together with each of them again.

Keys Day: Monday, February 15, 2010

My first Keys Day without Bill was so empty. That day had been so much fun for us—going out to dinner and exchanging cards... I went through all my greeting cards and pulled out all the ones I had received from Bill. Then I went through that pile and pulled out the most special ones to keep around my bedroom, so that I could read them often.

I soon found out that the last card I ever would receive from Bill had been for Keys Day 2009. I didn't know I could cry so hard.

Early March 2010

Julie was still helping me with paperwork, thank goodness. I gathered all the papers for my taxes, and she came over, went through all of them, and drove us to the tax place. I don't know what I'd do without her help.

Mid-March 2010

We heard at church that the priests were having a hard time with household duties, especially since "Mom" Betty's Parkinson's disease was progressing. "Mom" Betty was Father

Sam's mother, but they also added Father John as part of their family group. They were asking parishioners to occasionally bring over a meal for their family. I called Father John and told him I'd like to bring a meal; and he asked me to join them for dinner. That sounded nice to me and it would give me time to visit with them. Thus started our Thursday night dinners.

They teased me that I had become their adopted daughter and sister, and I liked the role.

The timeliness of this was also so good. March was the month that Bill and I would go on a cruise. How I missed this. And this month especially, since we had already booked a two-week Hawaiian cruise for our twenty-fifth anniversary. Debbie had cancelled it for me because I couldn't bear to make that call myself. Just the thought of it made me sick.

April 2010

At the first touch of spring, my faithful friend Beth was already checking out places for rummaging… and, of course, we'd have lunch later.

It turned out to be a bit chilly for many rummages, so we were usually forced to go to regular stores instead. I enjoyed getting out for a change, and I enjoyed the food. As usual, Beth was right about getting out. But it wouldn't last. By the time I was back home, I glued myself to a chair in the living room. And I thought and thought some more of Bill. And then I drank and drank some more… anything to numb the pain.

Thursday, May 20, 2010

The phone rang. It was the disability company, casually calling to tell me I had been denied coverage. It sparked a very sharp response from me. I told them, "It doesn't matter; I won't be here anyway," and I hung up the phone.

I started crying, thinking how people aren't very kind to widows. I was so mad I felt like tearing up the house. But I just cried instead.

A couple of minutes later I heard a knock on the front door. *Who can that be?* I wondered. I answered the door to see two policemen standing there. I tried to hide the fact that I was crying, so I stepped outside to see them, explaining my dogs were trying to get out.

Suddenly it was good cop, bad cop time. The bad cop said they had received a call from the disability company that I threatened to kill myself. I explained the story that I had lost my husband awhile back and was denied disability insurance. Yes, I was upset by them, and no, I shouldn't have said that.

The bad cop wasn't going for it. He said I obviously was still very upset since I was crying. Next they wanted to come into the house. Now I was scared. They asked if I was getting help for my emotions and I told them yes, I was seeing a psychiatrist, in fact I was seeing him that day.

They asked for his name and phone number. I gave them Dr. John's business card. The good cop went around the corner to call him, while the bad cop continued to talk with me. Now I was so nervous that I couldn't stop crying… not a good thing.

The good cop came around the corner, saying he had talked with Dr. John. They said I had three options: Number one was to have them take me to Dr. John right now, and Dr. John had agreed to this. Number two was they would take me to the county mental health facility for, I guess, mental people. I immediately said no to that one. The third, I still haven't figured out. I thought they said I could go to Dr. John at my scheduled session time. I chose that one, and quickly found out I misunderstood it, because now they were explaining to me that since I wasn't being cooperative, they were going to take me to the holding area.

I tried desperately to explain that I misunderstood option three and that I'd then rather have them take me to Dr. John's office. No luck. They again said since I hadn't cooperated, the choice had been made.

Crying, I asked them if I could change my clothes and take the dogs out first. They weren't happy with that, but agreed to it. The good cop went in the back yard with me, taking the dogs out. Then he followed me to the bedroom while I grabbed some clothes to change into. I went into the bathroom and I could tell he was right outside the door. How humiliating. I was almost done when he was telling me that this was taking too long, and we would have to go. I hurried and came out.

The bad cop talked with me for a while and then explained that the good cop was pulling the police car up to the house so the neighbors couldn't see as much. I appreciated that. But once outside, he explained I'd be handcuffed (*did I hear handcuffed?*) and I'd be put into the good cop's police car. Now I was crying again. *Me being handcuffed?* I thought. This couldn't be real. And they didn't just use the little plastic ties some police use; I was getting the large metal handcuffs that hurt. *How can this be happening to someone like me?* was the thought that kept running through my mind.

The bad cop then placed me in the back seat of the police car. I didn't know that the back seats of police cars didn't have cushions—they were only plastic. Ouch! I wasn't too comfortable with the handcuffs pressing against my back and the back of the seat. But I guess that was the point—this wasn't meant for pleasure. Luckily it was a short ride.

Now came the next step. As we entered the county building, there was an area with security police. They told me to remove my shoes and give them my purse. They removed my wallet, which they gave back to me, and then put the rest of my items in a bag that they duct-taped. The first thing I thought about was the book that Bill had received from Beth and Gary years ago entitled, *101 Items to Use with Duct Tape.* I'll bet this wasn't in the book.

First I had to go before a person asking me health questions. I figured they didn't want people to have a heart attack there, but I'm sure this was just a standard procedure. I made sure she had Dr. John's phone number, and asked her to call him.

The next window had someone who was telling me why I was being held and stuff like that. I don't remember much of this, because I was in I-can't-believe-this-is-happening mode and didn't listen very well.

The next window was—I couldn't believe it—the insurance person. *That's why I got my wallet back—to pay for all this,* I thought to myself. I had to show her my insurance card, and she told me I'd be billed for this visit. Now I was officially in I-can't-believe-this-is-happening mode.

Next they showed me my seat and told me to wait. I waited, and waited, and waited. I looked around the room and quickly realized I'd prefer to keep quiet and keep to myself. So I closed my eyes, pretending to sleep, but I was in deep thought, thinking about how easy it had been to end up in this place. I started thinking about how long they might keep me here.

What if I have to stay overnight? I wondered. Oh my gosh. Might I end up in a room alone, where someone could come in and violate me? Or a room with another person who might drive me more crazy? Or a unit with a whole lot of crazies?

Now I was picturing myself in the movie, *One Flew Over the Cuckoo's Nest.* I began to wonder, *How has my life changed so much in less than a year?* I sat and waited and worried.

Finally, a friendly nurse called my name and signaled me to come to her. I quickly went to the desk. She smiled and told me the doctor there had talked with Dr. John, and Dr. John had convinced him to release me to him. I'd need to go to his office immediately. That sounded great to me. I thanked her and immediately used the phone to call Roger. He said he'd come and pick me up.

I knew it would take a while, because he was on the other side of town and rush hour was starting. So, of course, I worried more. I kept thinking, *Please get me out of here before too much time goes by and they change their minds.*

Finally Roger was at the desk, telling the guards who he was here for. I headed to that area and they gave me back my belongings.

Dr. John's office was very close, so it didn't take long to get there. Roger would come back for me.

I stepped into Dr. John's waiting room. I sat for a while, a bit worried about what he was going to say about this. He came out of his office and looked at me, shaking his head and saying, "You never give up."

I followed him into his office, by now feeling quite embarrassed about what had happened. I told him the whole story.

Dr. John was so polite. He listened without giving my any grief. He agreed when I stated "I guess I should watch what I say to somebody on the phone." I was so thankful to Dr. John for getting me out of there. But we sadly talked about having to appeal the decision of the disability company.

Later I found out from Roger that normally, anyone going into the county holding site has to stay three days for evaluation. Oh my gosh—I hadn't realized just what Dr. John had gotten me out of. I emphatically told myself that I really did need to watch what I said from now on.

Amazingly, some good news came out of this. I guess I alarmed the person from the disability office enough to decide I did need the disability, because I soon got a letter from them stating my application was approved. I was glad, but quietly thought, *Maybe I could have found an easier way to do this.*

Friday, June 18, 2010

As soon as the calendar said June, I shivered. I couldn't believe it was almost a year since the accident; almost a year since I lost Bill.

Springtime used to be so wonderful. *Now, how am I going to get through these weeks and into July?* I followed the dates, waiting for June 18th, the night before the accident. I went to bed very early that night, hoping I'd sleep through it. But even though Dr. John had prescribed a couple of medications to help me sleep, I was still having trouble. When I couldn't sleep during the night, I'd often get up and go into the kitchen, either to watch the religious channel on the TV for a while, or to have something to eat, hoping this would calm me and tire me out.

Sometimes it worked. I'd get back in bed and fall asleep.

But not this night.

Late June 2010

Now my thoughts were reliving Bill's accident and every day Bill had spent in the hospital. I was rarely sleeping well. I was rarely eating. I was extremely anxious and very depressed. I didn't like these thoughts, but I also wanted to remember them as clearly as possible, as if this would keep me closer to Bill. I was crying all the time. I was drinking all the time. I was praying I could make myself sick enough to die and be with Bill.

Thursday, July 1, 2010

The calendar was really agitating me now. I was still focusing on all of Bill's days in the hospital. I couldn't believe a year had gone by. I had promised myself I wouldn't be on this earth for another year after Bill's passing.

I was already remembering July 1 as the anniversary of losing my mom three years earlier. That was a bad enough memory in itself, but now I had another countdown, to July 6th... the loss of Bill.

I told family and friends that the Fourth of July no longer existed for me. I wouldn't celebrate anything so close to the anniversaries of these deaths. I'd devote my time to praying, mainly about Bill, Mom, Dad... everyone. Reading the rosary daily gave me some comfort. Beth, Roger, Scott, and other friends were calling and e-mailing me to see how I was doing. It was an easy answer—horrible.

Sunday, July 4, 2010

I had wanted to stay home alone today. But because it was Sunday, I made a large bouquet of flowers from my yard to place near the altar at church. And then I visited the cemetery. I cried hard at both places. Then I headed home to stay alone, the way I wanted it.

I was reading a book on the life of Mother Teresa of Calcutta. That helped some. Petting my dogs helped some.

But I also kept up the crying and drinking. I hated the sounds of the fireworks as I was trying to sleep. These brought back too many memories that I was trying to bury in my mind.

Tuesday, July 6, 2010

I love you Bill. And I know you love me, too.
Alone, I said this over and over that day.
And, yes, I drank some more.

Thursday, July 8, 2010

At my appointment with Dr. John, I was crying so hard I could hardly talk. Dr. John gave his support to my grief, but he reminded me that I couldn't keep drinking so much. He said he understood why I was doing it, but went on to explain that drinking was keeping the medicines from acting as well as they should. I told him I'd try to slow down, but I knew I didn't want to.

Chapter Eleven

A New Focus

Sunday, July 11, 2010

There was now talk at church about renovating the rectory on the grounds of the church. It was a big, beautiful house; but it had been neglected for years. A discussion ensued at the church about money and help needed to do this job.

It started me thinking.

Monday, July 12, 2010

After more thinking, I decided there were three jobs that needed to be done.

Number one was helping Roger. He was receiving warnings from the city to complete work around his house and yard. The biggest job was to complete the addition to the back of his house. A couple of years back, a contractor had built it, but the electrical and the finish work had never been completed. Bill had been helping Roger with the electrical work, but he also hadn't finished. Roger didn't know much about that type of work, so he'd need an electrician for this. He had stopped work on much of his house because he had been laid off, so money was tight. The city had also given him deadlines on other things, including painting his garage.

Number two was my own house. The basement and hallway to the basement were looking quite shabby. It would need to be scraped and painted. I couldn't—and didn't want to—do it by myself.

Number three, and the biggest, was the rectory. I wanted to work on this for two reasons. One was that Bill had also done work in the rectory, and I knew I'd feel a real kinship with Bill, working where he had worked, with his tools. The other reason was that I loved the fathers' family. It was a real hardship having them in their current house. Father Sam wasn't able to be at church as often as needed, because it was difficult to leave Mom (Betty) alone too much of the time. The rectory was right on the grounds of the church. That would make a huge difference. If I was working there I'd be able to visit and help out with Mom more often. That would be good for her and me.

Everything hinged on getting someone who could help. I was still in contact with Dave and Jaci, and I knew that Dave had also been laid off. They were really tight for money, and I knew Dave had skills on home repair.

I hoped my plan would work…

First, I called the senior warden of the vestry. I told her my idea of getting Dave, me, and others (we hoped)) to take on the work at the rectory. I'd pay the workers, and the church would pay for other contractors and supplies. She loved the idea and said she'd talk with the priests. It only took a short time for her to call me back, saying they were so happy about the offer and wholeheartedly agreed.

Next, I needed to call Dave to see whether he'd agree. I told him, and after a quiet pause on the phone, I finally heard Dave. He was crying and saying he'd love to do the work.

Next was the call to Roger. I knew this would be tough, because Roger was a very proud person and had a hard time accepting help. As we talked, I explained this wasn't only for him; it would be good for me to focus on something besides losing Bill. He said he'd think about it and call me back.

Tuesday, July 13, 2010

It took until the next day, but Roger called and said he agreed.

I was ecstatic. I couldn't believe everyone had agreed. My plan was to put Roger's house as the priority, to get the city people off his back. But I knew the biggest project would be the rectory. My home could be done at the end.

Wednesday, July 14, 2010

Wednesday mornings were Bible study days. Dave was all for coming to the study, and then checking out the rectory.

As Dave and I toured the rectory, we saw there was quite a lot of work to be done. There were leaks all over the house, which meant tearing out a lot of the walls and ceilings. And the fathers wanted to add a full bathroom right next to Mom's room on the main floor.

Mid-July, 2010

The first part of the job was stopping the water from coming into the house and basement. We noticed the grading around the house was very poor in some areas, so we ordered a load of dirt and spread it around the house as needed. We had a basement company check out the property. They felt the grading was probably going to do the job, and we should wait and see how things went.

Next, we knew we needed to tear down a lot of walls and some ceilings. This was going to be more work than anticipated.

Dave gave me some wonderful news. His nephew, Tommy, who was also out of work, was willing to work with us. He had worked on a roofing crew and he had learned a lot from his father, a licensed contractor. He was in his twenties and strong—just what we needed.

I also thought of more help—David, my teenage nephew. He'd sure like to earn some cash before going back to school in the fall. And I could use Tommy and David at Roger's house, also.

Dave and I sighed with relief. We were in business.

Dr. John was glad I had found something to focus on.

Late July 2010

It was time to paint Roger's garage and house trim.

We couldn't have picked a hotter week to get started. The garage was mostly in the sun. I thought the paint might melt right off the wood in this heat. It did seem to be taking longer than usual to dry.

My poor nephew David wasn't so thrilled with this job. But, gee—no surprise—he loved the drives home when we would stop at McDonald's for a snack and I'd give him his pay for the day. After that, he was always ready to start another day.

Auntie wasn't such a good safety example, though. One day I decided to help paint under the garage soffit area. That meant painting right over my head. I was hurrying, because it was really a lousy job. I got my brush really full of paint and slopped it on. Big mistake. My eyes were wide open, watching what I was painting, when a huge drop of paint fell completely into my left eye socket.

I just about jumped off the ladder, yelling to anyone who could hear, "Help! I got paint in my eye!"

What scared me most was the amount of paint that went into the socket. I panicked, thinking, *What if the paint dries? I could go blind.* I grabbed a nearby bottle of water and started pouring it right into my eye. By then, everyone was at my side.

Dave had been a medic in Vietnam, so he immediately responded. He yelled to get the hose started, and to get some Q-Tips. He had me hold the hose while the water poured into my eye. It wasn't too bad when the water was still warm, but boy, it smarted when the water got cold. Periodically he'd tell me to stop so he could use a Q-Tip to dab at the spots that the hose was unable to get at. It all felt horrible, but I was calming down because I could still see.

Finally, my eye was clear. It was very red, but I could see. I was so thankful to everyone. It was a bit sore, but that didn't worry me. I knew it felt okay. Dave told me to check it first thing in the morning, just in case.

We started painting again, but for some reason, no one would let me paint the soffits again.

All this work was keeping me busy on weekdays, but the weeknights and weekends were still very rough. I even kept up the work at the rectory on weekends—anything to fill time.

Family and friends had pretty much given up their nightly ritual of visiting me. I missed that, but I understood. This had been a life-changing event for me, but I didn't expect everyone else to take care of me every day. Thank goodness for my dogs; they were such good company.

I continued to see Beth on most Saturday mornings, but even that was hard on both of us. She told me she didn't know what to do with me most of the time; that she wanted her old friend back, and she didn't know how to do that.

I told her that her old friend didn't exist anymore. I was a new person now; yes, I was still grieving and still depressed.

Beth, as well as many others, had hoped I'd have—I don't know—perked up by now. But that wasn't happening fast enough for them, and that became a problem.

I'd try to explain that I felt bad about that, but I wasn't ready, nor did I know if I'd ever be ready, to do a lot of the things I used to do.

And, yes, I was still drinking a lot and not eating much.

August 2010

Work continued full force through August. Now and again, we would get some of the church members to give us a hand. But it was mostly Dave, Tommy, David and me.

I was exhausted most of the time, but I refused to show it in front of the guys. I wanted to be part of the team. And it was working.

Now I was drinking beer during the day. My body hurt so much, and I'd get that knot in my stomach, so I'd bring a small cooler filled with beer. It helped me get through some of the rough days and it kept me a bit calmer—or so I told myself. I knew it wasn't good for me, but I didn't care about that.

Occasionally, I'd get a short visit from Father Russ when he was in the neighborhood. Father Russ is one of the most serene, content men I have ever known. He's as happy with a bowl of soup as with a steak. He was determined to help me get better; to make Jesus the center of my life, to help me be content with whatever happens in my life. That didn't seem so simple to me, but I appreciated his company and effort.

September 2010

Weekdays consisted of work, work, and more work. *Wow, what have I bitten off with all these plans?* I asked myself. My house could wait, but doing the rectory was a huge job. And David had gone back to school, so we were down to three workers most of the time. We were taking a break from Roger's house until we could find an electrician. At least the outdoor painting project was done.

I knew doing this work was good for me and for the people we were helping. But it sure was tiring. I still did my share of crying during the day, but I was usually in a room by myself so I wouldn't have to hold it in. And sometimes Dave would see me and come over to give me a hug. I enjoyed these hugs, because I so missed Bill's hugs. And some of the time I let myself feel proud for what we were accomplishing.

Dr. John and I agreed that the work was good therapy. I described how I was using a sledgehammer to knock down walls, and how I had even tried a jackhammer for a short while. I think he approved, mostly because I was socializing with more people than I had.

One of my not-so-favorite jobs was attic day. The old insulation had to be removed and fresh insulation put in. This was a horrible job. I was probably the one selected to go up into the attic because I had lost so much weight that it would be easier for me to crawl around the attic space. It was a very hot day, so the sweat was dripping from everywhere. I thought it would never end, but finally I put the last piece in place and was able to come down the ladder. Yeah!

Tommy had been sweeping the debris over the balcony to the patio, and Dave was hauling it to the dumpster. As I was brushing myself off, itching everywhere from the insulation, I realized my keys were not in my pocket. Oh my gosh—that is where I kept them all the time. I panicked. *What if they're in the attic someplace?* I'd never find them. But I had to try. I crawled back up and searched all over (and under) the insulation. I couldn't find them.

Now I was very worried. I went outside and thought, *What if they got swept up and put into the dumpster?* That was a disgusting thought. The huge dumpster was almost full with bags of dirty insulation. *Should I even attempt this?* I wondered. Yes, I had to. So I crawled into the dumpster and started ripping open all the bags, very methodically, making sure I didn't miss anything. Halfway through the process... yes! There were my keys. I couldn't believe I had actually found them.

I felt so good... tired and itchy, but good. This day was definitely done. Time for a beer.

Early October 2010

With the cooler weather coming, work on the rectory was mostly inside the house now. But the job kept getting more complicated. We had discovered that the kitchen had to be completely gutted, due to all the wetness and mold. We hadn't expected to do this much, but for safety reasons, it had to be done.

By now we were also using contractors, such as electricians, plumbers, concrete workers, landscapers, and HVAC specialists, to complete some of the work. It seemed endless.

The next step was having Dave and Tommy put up the drywall. Now I was getting nervous, because after that came mudding. I happened to know how to mud. The winter before Bill's accident, we (mostly Bill) had been working on gutting both of our existing bathrooms. During the process, the guys were starting to mud the seams of the drywall. They were not doing a good job. Our bathroom took so much work to get it looking okay that I told them no one would mud the main bathroom except me. It became a challenge, and I got pretty good at it.

Unfortunately, since I was good at it, now I was the master mudder on this project. I hated this job, but knew I'd probably have the best luck, so here I was. *Yuck,* was my only thought.

I especially hated doing ceilings, because it needed so much strength and I'd get a face full of dust when sanding it. But it was my job nonetheless, so I tried to stop whining, and started working on it.

Tuesday, October 26, 2010

I had been getting moody as the month went on. Anniversary time was here, and things were not getting any easier.

This year would have been our twenty-fifth anniversary. Bill had many times suggested that we have our vows renewed. I always found that sweet, but we never had any set plans to do it.

I guessed he would've suggested it for this anniversary. So I talked with Father Sam about officiating over an anniversary blessing for us. Father Sam was very touched, and said he indeed would do this. Another thing was that Bill had planned to have Dave as his best man. But Dave had been unable to attend our wedding, because he was in the Army, so Bill used another good friend as the best man.

So now, without Bill, I had Dave with me while Father Sam officiated the service at 2:00 p.m., our original marriage time. I cried through the entire service, but I knew it was the right thing to do.

Later that evening, I again drank our wedding champagne, Zonin, using our wedding glasses, and I spent time looking at wedding pictures. It was much harder this year, and I couldn't get myself to watch the video. I think it was because I wasn't in as much shock as the previous year. But I was still crying just as much.

Early November 2010

Work continued on the rectory. At least we had finally progressed to the upstairs bathroom. We were amazed how solidly this house was built. I was again using my sledgehammer to destroy a small linen closet in the upstairs bathroom. I'm sure Dr. John would say this was good therapy, because I was pounding as hard as I could, and I was just able to break through. Like most old houses, it had been built with plaster. But this house had one or two sheets of drywall on top of the plaster. I didn't even know they made drywall that long ago. I called Father John to tease him, saying, "Please explain to me why these people made a closet in an upstairs bathroom that could withstand an atomic bomb, before the bomb was ever created."

Late November 2010

Another birthday, another Thanksgiving. I enjoyed seeing my friends and relatives, but these holidays were hard without Bill. I realized I was still going through the motions, without much thought of my actions. Beth reminded me of this often.

Early December, 2010

Tommy got a job. We were so glad for him, but sad for us. We were breaking up the trio. Dave and I sure would have liked to use him to help finish the jobs. We enjoyed a final lunch, drank to Tommy, and watched him leave. Darn... more work for us. More beer.

Mid-December 2010

Winter weather was arriving fast. First we had ice, then a lot of snow. One day as I was leaving the rectory, forgetting about the ice below the snow, I tried to turn out of the parking lot to leave, but my car didn't turn as much as I wanted it to. I went up and over a snow bank. I tried to get out going back and forth, but no luck.

Dave was still in the rectory, so I called him on my cell phone. He'd be out in a minute, so I got the shovel out of my trunk and started to try to dig my car out. It looked pretty impossible; my car had really gotten stuck on the other side of the snow bank. Dave also tried shoveling and directing my back-and-forth movements of the car. No luck.

We didn't know what to do. Luckily, a man driving a truck pulled into the lot. He had a chain in the back of his truck and used it to pull me out. I was thanking everyone! I guess it was good to get stuck in a church parking lot. I gave God a thank-you also.

Late December 2010

It was time for another Christmas tree. This time Beth said they wouldn't get a tree for me; I'd have to go with them. There was no way I could go to the lot and watch them cut down trees. That memory was with Bill alone. So instead, I called Billy. He was a tough one, also. He said he'd help me get a tree, but I'd need to go along.

They had me cornered. Okay, I went with Billy and we went to a nearby lot. Of course I picked the first tree I saw, right next to Billy's truck. Time to go home!

It was a nice tree, but boy, was it expensive. We had been cutting our own trees for so long, I was shocked at how much the pre-cut ones were now.

With the tree up in my living room now, I put up a few more decorations than the year before, and it was done.

Friday, December 24, 2010

Again, I loved having the family come to my house for Christmas Eve. It was hard without Bill, but I knew it was easier being with them than being alone. I hoped they knew that also.

I missed going to midnight Mass, as we always had done, but I felt too tired and too emotional to do that now.

Saturday, December 25, 2010

I chose to again join Scott's family at his church for Christmas Day. The kids seemed to enjoy having me there, and I got to see some of our old friends that came from St. Andrew's. It was very emotional, though.

Early January 2011

We were getting close to finishing the rectory. A few more weeks should do it. And I was glad, because we could then turn our attention back to Roger's projects.

I was also enjoying reading some of the books that I got from the Catholic supply store. I needed some spiritual help, and these were working. I especially liked some of the biographical books on the saints.

Chapter Twelve

A Hard Fall

Saturday, January 15, 2011

Billy called to say he was stopping by tonight. It was strange that he didn't mention a reason why; he usually did. But no problem... I always liked to see him.

Later that evening, Billy came into the house with Julie. Now I felt confused. They said they wanted to talk with me.

We sat at the kitchen table and they started talking. They explained that they had concerns about my drinking, and if I didn't get a handle on it, they wouldn't be coming around anymore.

We were all crying. They told me they loved me, but they couldn't take seeing me this way. I didn't know what to say or do. Drinking had become a huge bandage for me. I knew Dr. John wasn't happy that I was drinking so much, but I hadn't realized the kids were so aware of it. I didn't know it showed so much. And I didn't know how I was going to be able to give up my so-called coping mechanism. I wasn't even sure I wanted to stop.

We said goodbye and they left. I poured one drink and stopped.

January had turned very cold. The ground was frozen solid outside, so taking the dogs out wasn't much fun. But it was time for bed, so that meant one more trip outside for the doggies.

Poor Lady… she wanted to explore everything in the yard, but her rope was always getting stuck on something. Tonight it was stuck between two rocks. I was carefully walking toward the area, because it was icy. I bent over to get the rope unstuck. As I pulled the rope loose, the rope became taut and it started pulling me forward.

My reaction was to pull back… and then I have a faint memory of the rope becoming slack. My next memory was of rolling over some rocks on the ground.

I didn't know it yet, but I had been unconscious for an unknown period of time. I could feel my head was hurting, so I knew I had fallen, but I didn't quite remember it.

Both dogs were right near me, so I slowly got up and we headed back into the house. I remember thinking about how very tired I felt, so without further thought, I quickly set my alarm for Mass the next day and went to sleep.

Sunday, January 16, 2011

The alarm woke me up. I felt a pain on my face and on my eyes. I touched the edge of my eye and quickly let go. *Ick.* It felt like a bulge, and it hurt.

I got out of bed in a panic and looked into the bathroom mirror. Oh my gosh, I looked like a raccoon. Both my eyes were black and bulging. I couldn't believe it.

I remembered falling the night before, but couldn't understand how I had fallen on my eyes without having any other scratches or bruises on my face.

There was no church for me that day. I first fed the dogs and took them out. Then I took an ice pack out of the freezer, sat in a chair in the living room, and put the ice pack on my eyes.

The last thing I wanted to do on this cold day was to apply ice to my eyes, but I had no choice. I did think about going to the emergency room, but I figured they would probably just give me the same advice—to ice my eyes.

Monday, January 17, to Saturday, January 22, 2011

The rest of the week was very fuzzy. I know I kept icing my eyes every day and they were starting to look a little better. And they didn't hurt very much.

I'm unsure of who I saw or talked to during this week. I do remember Scott and Debbie coming over one evening, and they also told me to go to the hospital, but I told them I was icing my eyes.

Debbie even called her sister-in-law, a nurse. She also suggested both things—go to the ER and ice my eyes. So I thought I had it under control by icing them.

Wrong.

Sunday, January 23, 2011

Again, the alarm awoke me for church. But this time I received a very sharp pain across my forehead—the type that almost knocks you to the floor. *Do I realize now I should go to the hospital?* I asked myself.

No. I put ice on my eyes again and sat in the living room. I have no more memories of that day.

Monday, January 24, 2011

I don't remember getting up, but I do have a memory of going to the computer and checking my e-mails. I even replied to Wanda about having dinner together that night at my house.

I have no other memories until one of a short awakening as Shannon sat down on the bed next to me. Startled, I looked at her, but again, that's all I remember.

Shannon explained to me later that she had called the house and I wasn't making any sense, and then she heard a dial tone. So she called back, but this time I didn't pick it up. She was just getting off work, so she came to my house.

My next memory found me in the West Allis Memorial Hospital emergency room. Family members were all around my bed, staring at me. There was a doctor explaining to me that he was a neurosurgeon. He was talking about tests that I had just had, which I didn't remember.

I was dressed in a hospital gown, and I was starting to realize that many hours had gone by. The doctor was explaining about the different types of hematomas and that I had two of the most dangerous type—subdural hematomas—and a cracked skull. I heard him say, "A blow to the back of the head equals raccoon eyes." That explained a lot.

He went on to explain that normally, with a situation like this, he'd be operating on my head to relieve the pressure on the hematoma. But mine was too large and it was situated in a bad location—one side was too close to my carotid artery and the other side was too close to my spinal column fluids, which could paralyze me.

I was very confused and felt like I was in a dream. He went on to explain that if he did surgery, that would kill me, so he was going to wait and see if the hematomas would decrease on their own. But he said that could kill me also, because all the bruises throughout my head might leak fluids into the large hematoma on the lower backside of my head.

He continued, saying the larger hematoma was in the sight center of the brain, and this would be affecting my eyes. I looked around realizing that, yes, everything was blurry and distorted.

He said when someone takes a fall like I did, the brain is like Jell-O, bouncing around and hurting other parts of the brain.

The second subdural hematoma I had was above my left eye. He said that one wasn't as dangerous, because it was more likely to drain.

I couldn't believe I was hearing all this. It sounded very serious, but I wasn't especially scared. My thoughts were usually about wanting to die anyway, so I felt a little happy; maybe this was what Jesus had planned for me. I tried not to smile.

Someone in the room started asking me questions about a living will. I was mad at myself. I had planned to take care of these types of things, especially after what had happened to Bill. I explained no, I didn't have one.

He then asked me if I wanted extra care to keep me alive. I knew I was going to answer no, but I stopped a moment. It was strange to be asked that question when the situation really called for it.

I was thinking about what I should answer, and said no, without any other thought. Someone behind me remarked that I only said no because I was depressed. Again I lost consciousness.

The next thing I remember is being taken into my ICU room. I told the nurse I had to go to the bathroom, expecting she'd help me get up to do that. Wrong. She slid a bedpan under me. Another new experience. *Ick.*

The next step wasn't much better. I started to notice that I had needles and cords connecting me to a machine. Looking at that machine caused me to shiver. It reminded me of Bill's machines in his ICU room. This was now really becoming a nightmare. I was pinned to this bed; it was too similar to how Bill had been pinned to his bed.

Some of the family joined me in my room. I was also often visited by nurses, who asked me the same questions over and over to see if I was coherent. At first I couldn't figure out why they were doing that, but I finally caught on. I also guessed they wanted me to stay awake. Maybe that was safer.

Tuesday, January 25, 2011

I lay in the ICU, near death, as I was told later. I knew I had pain in my head, especially my eyes and forehead. I was extremely uncomfortable because of the needles and cords connecting me to my vital records machine. My recurring memories of Bill in the hospital made it all so worse. A claustrophobic feeling was growing in me.

Wednesday, January 26, 2011

During the day I was told by the doctor on call that I'd be assigned to a psychiatrist to follow up on my care. I didn't like this, because I didn't want to start with someone new; I wanted Dr. John to continue to be my psychiatrist. So I called Dr. John to let him know I was in the hospital. He said he couldn't see me unless he was consulted by the doctor assigned to me. I told him I'd ask the doctor to consult with him.

Family and friends were so sweetly coming by to check on me. I guess it was good news that I had made it three days without more complications. But that night the family seemed to all join together, insisting I take better care of myself, and to see whomever the doctor on call wanted me to see.

I know they were correct, but I felt too pressured, and I was fighting their attempts to help me. I was having trouble concentrating and seeing, and I hadn't even been able to leave my bed alone yet. This was too much to take. I responded with a lot of crying.

Thursday, January 27, 2011

By day four I awoke with more strength. I was comforted in understanding that my family and friends were taking care of my dogs.

A rehab technician came into my room, talking about the start of rehab, and I instantly decided I was going to work very hard, hoping to get out of the hospital sooner. The tech was there to explain things to me, but I insisted I was ready to get up and work on some of her exercises. She agreed and helped me up. I was shocked at just how weak and unstable my movements were. But I was encouraged by the tech. She said I was moving way ahead of schedule and she'd be back the next day. Good—finally some news I wanted to hear.

As the evening approached, I was surprised that Dr. John came in to visit me. He explained to me that he was here as a friend, not a doctor. He had not yet received notification of consulting, so as a friend, he wanted to see how I was doing.

What a nice man. We talked. I kept asking his advice on different things, and he'd keep reminding me he was here as a friend. Okay, I'd wait. I was just glad to know he was watching my care.

Friday, January 28, 2011

I got more good news—I was to be transferred to St. Luke's for rehab. Daily CT scans showed my hematoma hadn't decreased yet, but this was good news, because it hadn't increased any. They felt I should get more rehab, and I was all for that.

What I wasn't ready for was the bumpy ride in the ambulance. All the way from West Allis to St. Luke's, I had to hold my head up or it would have been very painful.

They wheeled my ambulance bed into the rehab unit. I was in such pain above my left eye, and my vision was very bad. I was having double vision, and everything looked like it was moving around. It made me nauseated.

Because it was late evening, everything was dark and quiet, and I was nervous about every noise I heard. I felt very alone and scared. But soon a nurse and doctor came into the room. They explained I was in so much pain because they were still waiting for my hospital records to arrive from West Allis. Until then, they couldn't give me any medications. That sounded crazy to me, but there was no choice but to wait.

After what seemed like a couple of hours, they finally brought in a medication pole and IV lines. The pain eased up some as I tried to fall asleep.

Saturday, January 29, 2011

The next morning started early. My head and eye pain were still very severe. They brought in breakfast and I tried to clean up as best I could. Then I rested for a while, until the technicians came in to start my exercise program.

I sure didn't feel like rehab that morning, but I wanted to get out as soon as possible, so I worked as hard as I could. I knew in order to go home I'd have to improve enough to be able to take the dogs out.

The techs created complicated obstacle courses for me to work on, because I kept explaining to them I'd need to walk on uneven ground to take the dogs out. Between my bad eyes and lack of coordination, these courses were very difficult to maneuver, but I was trying my best.

A psychologist came in to talk with me. She got my background, and I explained that I had been seeing Dr. John and wanted to continue with him. She didn't see anything in the charts about that, which upset me further.

My nurse explained to me that I wasn't to get up on my own. If I did, an alarm would go off at the nurses' station. This felt so weird, but I completely understood. They didn't want people falling in their rooms.

I also found out there was a camera in my room someplace, because they knew what I was doing at all times. Boy, did I feel like a germ in a Petri dish. I had to call a nurse to help me with anything, including going to the bathroom. I definitely had to let go of my inhibitions. There was no privacy here… and that was probably good.

Sunday, January 30, 2011

I was worried that Sunday would be just a day of rest, but I was wrong. My nurse explained that a chart on the wall showed the time for different rehabs and consultations from staff. I let her know I was having difficulty seeing most things, but I'd give it a try. I asked to have someone bring in communion for me. I also found a Mass on channel EWTN.

Beth and Gary came to visit at the same time a rehab tech came in to test my coordination and eyesight. I thought they would have to wait, but it worked out okay, because they were allowed to stay in my room and watch.

The tech had me going through a series of tests, such as checking my hand and pen coordination, and she also gave me numbers to write down that I had to add or multiply.

The tech seemed to feel I was doing pretty well. I sure didn't feel that way. I could hardly write and could hardly see what I wrote.

There was plenty of work ahead of me.

Monday, January 31, 2011

The day was full of physical therapy and occupational therapy. My poor eyesight made it so much harder. By the end of the day I asked if I could have a shower. It was the strangest shower I ever had. The nurse had me sit on a bench and do all the chores of starting the water, putting soap on a wash cloth, and everything else, while she stood there and watched. She was checking to see whether I was coordinated enough to handle these tasks. I finished with flying colors. But I didn't know which I felt more like—a little kid, or an elderly person.

That night, a horrible snowstorm was coming our way. The weatherman was threatening quite a few inches of snow, but I still got a few visitors, including Roger. At least he was close to home. Everyone was taking turns letting the dogs out at my house.

Tuesday, February 1, 2011 through Thursday, February 3, 2011

Dr. John stopped in on an official hospital visit early in the morning. He explained he had finally been contacted to consult on my case. He calmed me down just by being there. I felt bad, though, because he had had to drive in that snowstorm to get to St. Luke's. He explained that I'd also continue to be followed by a staff therapist until I was released. Afterward, he'd still be my doctor. I thanked God for that.

Wednesday, February 2, 2011

When I awoke Wednesday morning, I found out that a large portion of the staff were unable to come in because of the snow. There wasn't any staff for therapy today, so it was promising to be a long day. And because my eyesight was so bad, there wasn't much for me to do. I sat on my bed and watched the weather all day long. It was a long one.

Thursday, February 3, 2011

I continued to slowly regain more of my strength and coordination. By afternoon, the tech came to get me for my exercise session. As we were walking down the hallway (with the usual belt strap around me for the tech to hold onto) I suddenly realized I wasn't shuffling like I had been doing. I was actually walking with my normal gait. I was thrilled and pointed it out to the tech. She watched and agreed. It was great news.

The tech made my obstacle course even more difficult, to test my coordination. It was a lot of work, but I was getting better at it.

Next I was tested in a pretend house with a kitchen and bedroom. I had to fold clothes and I even had to make a grilled cheese sandwich. I passed both tests just as Dave Ronn came in to see me.

We had a long hug. He said he had been quite worried, because I hadn't shown up at the rectory and I wasn't answering my cell phone. I explained I couldn't recharge my cell phone in the hospital, and I couldn't call long-distance from the hospital room phone. We had a nice visit, and we knew I'd be getting out soon.

Chapter Thirteen

Home Again

Friday, February 3, 2011

All the doctors and staff assigned to my case had a meeting and decided that, if my CT scan was okay, they would release me that day. I had the scan and anxiously awaited the results. The doctor came in and gave me the good news—there was a slight improvement to the hematoma, so I'd be released.

I called Roger to come and get me. Thank goodness, I was going to see my dogs this afternoon. But now came the big test. *Will I be able to take them out without falling down myself?* I wondered. I wished it was later in the winter season, so we wouldn't have snow for such long a time yet.

Roger stayed around to take the dogs out. That gave me a reprieve until the following day. The snow and ice looked deadly to me.

Saturday, February 4, 2011

The big test was here. I slowly got the dogs ready to go out. Lady was a saint. She didn't get stuck on anything and quickly returned with the leash. Deogee was always quick to come back. I had tackled my first outing.

The next trip outside was a little more complicated. I had to walk outside a bit to get Lady's leash untangled. It was going to be a long winter.

Scott and the family came over, bringing me food, and they took out the dogs in the evening. I felt a little more relaxed with the help. I headed to bed after they left.

Sunday, February 5, 2011

Julie reminded me that next weekend would be her wedding in Shiocton, and she wanted me to attend all three days. That scared me to death. I was so weak yet, and my eyesight was still very bad. On top of that, I knew it would be very emotional, not having Bill there. She told me it was so important to her that I be there, because I stood for the best memories of her dad. I understood and agreed to go.

Monday through Thursday, February 6-9, 2011

I was trying to relax, doing rehab, and getting things ready for the wedding weekend. I was so nervous. And I hated to leave my poor dogs again.

Friday, February 10, 2011

Billy drove me up to Shiocton. They had a hotel booked, so the guests would be all together. That night was the wedding rehearsal and dinner. At least I didn't have to do much besides sit in the pew and eat dinner. That alone tired me out.

Saturday, February 11, 2011

I drove with Shannon's family to the church. As the attendees were lining up to go down the aisle, Julie let me know that Jessica and I would be going down the aisle first so Jessica could light a candle near Bill's picture.

I know Julie waited until the last minute to tell me that because it would be more likely that I'd say yes. Very nervously, Jessica and I started down the aisle. I was praying I wouldn't mess up and embarrass her. The next step was to stop near a picture of Bill and not cry. I managed to hold it in until I got to my pew.

After all the bridesmaids were finished, Julie came down the aisle with Billy, looking beautiful, but crying. That started me crying again. Luckily she got it together and had a wonderful wedding ceremony with Bob.

With the lights dimmed and so many people, entering the reception hall was a bit scary. I kept hanging on to people so I wouldn't trip on chair legs.

The family was all there—including the Bonchers. The music started and the wedding party came out. The next song was for Bob and his mom. I stared at Julie, worried about how she must be feeling without her dad there.

When the song ended, Julie came to me to let me know the whole family was going to dance a tribute song for Bill. "Will you dance with David?" she asked. (Again, she was smart enough to wait until right before we had to get up to ask me). I said yes, and as we got up, the DJ started to play, "Old Time Rock'n' Roll."

Tears streamed down my cheeks as I remembered a week or so earlier Julie had asked me what were a couple of the dance songs Bill and I had enjoyed.

I turned around and saw that, yes, the whole family was up dancing. It was pretty dark on the dance floor, so I decided "What the heck? I'll dance for Bill." Partway through the song, I turned and saw Julie dancing with Bob. She was crying quite a lot. I walked over to her and the two of us hugged and cried. Then we started dancing together. It was a wonderful tribute, but oh, how hard.

Sunday, February 12, 2011

Guests gathered at the hotel for a brunch before returning home. This time I rode with Scott and his family. That helped me relax. By the time I got home, I was ready for bed. Roger had the dogs until tomorrow, so I was able to relax and get some much-needed sleep.

Monday, February 13, 2011

As I awoke, I realized that I was back home. I started to think about all that I had done. Many things had gone better than I had expected. It had been wonderful to see Julie's happy face. It had been wonderful to be there. If only Bill had been there too. Maybe he was.

Roger brought the dogs home in the afternoon. What a bit of joy those two dogs bring me.

Mid-February, 2011

Life at home was strange. I couldn't drive because of my eyesight. I prayed it would improve some.

I was having pretty good luck taking the dogs out, but it was sure scary. I felt thankful every time I got back into the house. Susan next door was driving me to my doctor appointments.

I also had a new rule—I wasn't allowed to drink any alcohol because of my brain injury. I was told even a little amount could cause more damage. I wasn't missing the alcohol itself, but I was missing the numbing effect it had on me.

During this time, since I was no longer drinking, I was unable to look at any more photograph books or even think about the good times that Bill and I had shared. I'd even have problems looking at framed photographs that I had looked at so many times. Any time I'd see or think about the good times, I'd get such a knot in my stomach. That would cause me to think about the bad times—Bill's time in the hospital and his death. This upset me immensely; now the good time memories also felt stolen from me, and there was nothing I could do about it.

During all this time, while I had been in the hospital, Dave had been doing finishing touches around the rectory. Now there were only a couple of things left to do. He knew I'd like to be there before the final completion, so he picked me up one day, and after doing a couple of minor jobs, we were all done.

The rectory was ready to be blessed by Father Sam. They chose a Sunday so all the parishioners would be present, and to my surprise and delight, it was dedicated to Bill. I was so proud. Our goal had been reached. The family would be able to move in. I was so glad for Mom Betty.

Late February, 2011

Following my hospital stay, Billy and Julie had asked if they could go with me to one of Dr. John's appointments. I said I'd check with him, and he said if that's what I wanted, it would be okay with him. So the three of us went together to a session.

Billy and Julie explained their concerns to Dr. John and said they thought I should also be seeing a therapist. I didn't say much, in order to give Billy and Julie time to talk.

At my next session with Dr. John, he decided on two courses of action. One, I was to attend two weeks of Intensive Out Patient sessions with attention to drinking. I wasn't too happy with this. The thought of a group session upset me, but Dr.

John didn't give me a choice on this one. The second thing was, after I finished the sessions, I was to be assigned to a therapist. I was agreeable to this, but I was worried about whether I'd like the person.

Friday, March 11, 2011

I was really nervous about my first appointment with Gregg, my new therapist, but he surprised me. The first session went well. He had a different style from Dr. John, but that probably provided a good balance.

Gregg dug deep into the things that bothered me. He also had more time to do that, because this was a forty-five-minute session. Dr. John had about a half hour or so, and he always needed time to discuss how my medications were doing. I was still having trouble sleeping, so that was a discussion I had with both Dr. John and Gregg.

Late March 2011

It was tax time again, and Julie once again was helping me. The whole family was taking time to see me. Billy and Scott's family were stopping by the house to visit with me and to take care of projects, and Shannon and the grandkids stopped occasionally for a visit. Roger was coming often, as was Beth. I felt so blessed to have such a good family and friends. I enjoyed their company.

April 2011

My eyes were still not improving, and this worried me more all the time. Before, at least I was able to drive where I wanted. Now I needed a ride from someone, so I mostly stayed home.

Luckily a nice couple from church would pick me up and take me to church with them. But I had to give up going to Roman Catholic churches, where Father Russ was saying Mass. I had been enjoying this, because he was going to a lot of the older churches on the east side. I had never before been in many of those huge, old, beautiful churches. And I felt comfortable because there weren't many parishioners at these Masses.

It was very upsetting that I could hardly read anything. Before the accident, that had been one of my diversions. I mostly read religious-based books, and they were calming to me. Now I could read a page or two with good light, but then the print would get dark and blurry. This wasn't good.

May 2011

Thank goodness, Beth and I were starting to rummage again. That felt very good. It got me out, and we would have our Mexican lunch.

It had been a long, cold winter.

Early June 2011

I was seeing an eye therapist at West Allis Memorial Hospital, and she was giving me hints on some things that might make my sight a little better. I bought a very bright lamp for my kitchen table. This now became the place where I could do paperwork.

I was starting to see a little better, so I decided to take a short drive to the store. I was very nervous. My eyesight sure wasn't perfect, and my depth perception and peripheral vision were worse, so I compensated for that.

I continued to take more trips in my car. I was becoming more confident, and my eyesight seemed to be improving some. Being able to get out on my own was a huge and much-needed accomplishment.

My accident, though, had caused me to be even more isolated than before. I didn't get much enjoyment out of seeing people when I couldn't see very well. And this time of year I used to enjoy the beginning of gardening. Now I could hardly see the plants.

Yes, I was feeling even sorrier for myself.

Chapter Fourteen

New Friends, New Losses

Mid-June 2011

In January, Father Sam had decided (or hoped) I'd agree to be the treasurer of St. Edmund's. That had been put on hold during my recovery time. Since my eyes were a little better now, Dick, the senior warden, was going to show me the books so I could take over this job.

I had mixed feelings about this. I didn't know whether I really wanted to get back into doing paperwork, and more importantly, I was worried about whether my eyes were good enough to read the information.

Dick and I met, and the work didn't seem too bad. But complications would be coming soon. I wasn't only to be the treasurer of the church, but also of the newly formed preschool. I'd need to start keeping a set of books for each place.

But it felt good to be participating in church events again. I had been afraid my damaged eyes had put an end to that.

Mid-June 2011

Work had been stalled at Roger's house because the electrical had still not been completed. I asked Dave to try to find an electrician we could use. He came up with a possibility, and Roger agreed to the choice.

The electrician came a couple of times and the inspector approved the work. We could finally work on the drywall and mudding.

The timing was going to be difficult with Roger's and Dave's schedules. Roger was having trouble sleeping, so he got up late. And he was very concerned about getting his vegetable garden started. He had a huge garden, and it would take a lot of work.

Dave preferred starting early and leaving for home early. So the two schedules didn't leave much time for work. We could only get in two to three hours a day. This was going to be a long project.

I wanted to concentrate on Roger's work at his house, but it was approaching the two-year anniversary of Bill's accident and my mind was definitely on him. I was trying to cope with both, but it was hard. How I wanted to join Bill.

I again started having a beer here and there.

Late June 2011

Because I was having such difficulty dealing with this anniversary, I was sometimes seeing Gregg, the therapist, twice a week. I was still seeing Dr. John once a week.

I found it too difficult balancing life on earth with my thoughts of heaven with Bill. This time of year was just too hard for me.

But I had a new diversion. Starting up the new preschool at St. Edmund's wasn't without some problems. Father Sam, Father John, and I had a few discussions regarding the issues and we had the idea of bringing in someone new. The name of Helene soon became prominent.

Once Helene was on board, she, Kelly, and I started dedicating hours of our time to the achievement of the preschool. And Helene and I were fast becoming friends. She had recently become estranged from her husband, and, although it was a very different situation from mine, we had some common threads in our lives. We often said the same things, and had some things in common. She was good company for me during the week.

Wednesday, July 6, 2011

It was the two-year anniversary of Bill's death. Father John did a Mass in the chapel for the remembrance of Bill on the date of his death.

Will this time of year ever get easier? I wondered. I was sure it wouldn't. Family and friends were, understandably, no longer coming over as often, and being alone was becoming the norm.

My thoughts were, of course, still cemented with Bill.

Mid-July, 2011

My eye therapy at West Allis was now done. The therapist suggested I see a neurological optometrist to further work on my eyes. There was a doctor very close to my house, so I made an appointment. I went through a lengthy series of tests and then saw the doctor. Unfortunately, she didn't see too much improvement. I was surprised, because I felt I could see better. She explained that I probably regained some of the peripheral damage, but my two eyes were still not lining up as they should.

During my hospital time, the doctor had thought I should block off one eye at a time so I could see more clearly. That seemed to work at the time, but not as much now. The current specialist said not to do that, because it wasn't letting my eyes try to heal themselves. I found that to be true; my eyesight was better using both eyes again. This was a pleasant surprise.

Late July 2011

The work on Roger's room was slowly moving forward. Half of the drywall was now up, so I could start mudding in some areas.

At home, I decided I wanted to paint an oil painting of our back yard, showing all my flowers, but in the back I wanted to show Bill splitting wood in front of his wall of wood. I had seen Bill splitting wood so many times through the years that I wanted a memory of it. In the sky, I'd paint a dove—the Holy Spirit—shining light down on Bill, just as his last day on earth had been.

Now, to get started...

August 2011

At Roger's house, all the drywall was up. I was able to do more mudding, but that was a slow process. Roger had to keep some of their belongings in the room, so to sand any of the mud meant we would have to put up plastic to keep the dust down. It wasn't the easiest way to do this job, but that's the way it would need to be done.

At home I was starting work on my oil painting. I had found a picture of Bill using his splitter in one of our photo albums. It helped to have a picture of the splitter.

Now with the picture drawn, I could start painting. It was more emotionally draining than I had expected. To steady my hand—and stomach—I took a drink every time I spent some time painting.

Scott and his family were still coming to visit about once a week, food in hand. These were very calming evenings for me.

September 2011

Mudding a couple days a week was still going on at Roger's house. Dave was now helping Roger with some of the outdoor projects that Roger needed to complete before winter.

I was putting the finishing touches on my painting. In some ways I liked it a lot; in some ways not. But I decided that once I got my stairwell and basement painted, I'd hang the painting in the hall going downstairs. I wanted it someplace I could see it, but not all the time. When I looked at it I'd cry, thinking about Bill.

The treasurer's job at St. Edmund's was taking up more time than I had hoped. Money continued to be short, so I had to be very careful. Sometimes I got very tense, being responsible for such a tight budget.

October 2011

As Halloween and Terry's birthday approached, only a couple of weeks were left before we needed to stop work at Roger's house again. Roger and Terry both enjoy putting up many decorations inside and outside, and they enjoy giving treats to the trick-or-treaters; so I wouldn't be able to do any more sanding for a while.

The break from Roger's house was good for me, because I wanted some of my own time for our anniversary. I kept it very quiet, between Bill and me, as I knew the family would worry about me still focusing on our anniversary—the twenty-sixth now. Back to my Zonin to celebrate our wedding reception alone.

Dr. John and Gregg informed me of two diagnoses for me. One was complicated grief, in which a person is stuck in grief. This type of grief takes more time to move through. The other diagnosis was PTSD, or Post Traumatic Stress Disorder.

That's why I kept remembering the hospital time with Bill over and over.

They suggested I start a third weekly therapy session with Carla, a therapist specialized to work on a new therapy called Eye Movement Desensitization and Reprocessing (EMDR). It's an aid to help calm down traumatic memories. I decided to go with their suggestion. The suffering I felt was endless. And many times, I preferred to think about ending this lifetime on earth.

Early November 2011

We were able to fit in a couple of days of sanding at Roger's house while Dave again was helping Roger outside. But after that, we would need to wait until after Christmas to do any more work.

I had my first session with Carla. The EMDR therapy usually is done with flashing lights, but because of my bad eyesight, she decided on a tapping method instead.

The first session was horrible. Carla sat behind me, explaining she would be tapping me on different places of my back. She was tapping me softly, and I quickly held memories of Bill hugging me. I got severely anxious. I was upset the whole rest of the day.

The next session was even worse. Carla tapped on my knees while I was to remember over and over a scene from Bill's hospital time. I sobbed so hard it was hard to recover. I went home and drank quite a bit.

Dr. John, Gregg, and Carla discussed this and decided that Carla would need to go much slower with me.

I found it hard to believe I now had a team of a doctor and two therapists.

Late November 2011

Beth suggested that for my birthday, she and Gary would take me to a Mexican bar/restaurant that we liked for dinner. That sounded good to me, so I also told Roger about it. At the restaurant, Roger and Terry showed up. It was a pretty nice evening. At least I didn't cry this time.

Then came Thanksgiving. It was still good to have the family come to our house for the big meal.

Early December 2011

A lawsuit had erupted back in 2008 between St. Edmund's Anglican Church and the Milwaukee Episcopal diocese, with each saying the property of St. Edmund's was theirs. The suit was now coming to a conclusion. Father Sam had a tight case showing the grounds belonged to us, but now, the news wasn't looking good. A judge was put on the case who visibly favored the Episcopal Church. Even though Father Sam had written proof that we should win the case, it was ignored by the judge, who stated, "A deed isn't worth anything." The judge even worked out a scenario that kept us from being able to appeal his verdict. The parish was very anxious about the future of St. Edmund's.

Mid-December 2011

This year I invited Billy, Julie, and Bob to help me pick out a tree. It was easier having more people around me because we were all making conversation. We went to Home Depot and Bob quickly found the one to buy.

We went back to my house to put up the tree. I had promised them a dinner afterward. What a deal. They picked pork chops, and they sure seemed to like it. I was so glad, because I didn't cook very often anymore.

Friday, December 16, 2011

Father Russ called. He'd have time for a visit today, and I was glad. One or the other of us always brings up having soup. That's all Father Russ really wants. He is content with so little on this earth.

But this time the conversation got rough on me. Father Russ brought over a series of articles on "How to Pray." He was explaining to me the parts of the article that were most important, and then shared some concerns with me about how I was praying. I've shared a lot about myself with him, so he probably was right—but it was still very hard to hear. I knew he was just trying to help me, but it left me crying and feeling hopeless that I wasn't doing anything right.

Friday, December 23, 2011

As I was looking at the Christmas cards that people have sent me, I noticed that Gail and Bob had given me their cell phone numbers. Yes, I'd call them; it had been way too long. I couldn't believe I got ahold of Gail right away and learned that they were in town this week. They suggested we get together for lunch. It was so good seeing them.

Saturday, December 24, 2011

Christmas Eve was again at my house. It so helped that the family wanted to come to our house. I couldn't imagine facing it without them.

Sunday, December 25, 2011

On Christmas Day, I again went to church with Scott's family at St. Peter's. Afterward, I had a surprise invitation from Helene. She said she was going to have a small dinner party with her brother and family and would like me to come. That sounded good to me, and it was. I felt very welcome, and I sure enjoyed her cooking. We had become good friends.

I left a little early to get over to Beth's house. Beth, Gary, the girls, and their boyfriends were watching a Packers game. It was a good end to an emotional day.

Early January 2012

Father Sam held a meeting after church. Our worst fears were true. St. Edmund's had lost the lawsuit, and we would have to vacate the church, the rectory, and the preschool building.

This news hit me heavily. I thought the church members would stay together, but the site of the church and rectory had great ties to Bill for me. I had spent so much time and money redoing the rectory in Bill's memory. It just seemed I was losing more and more.

I started doing more drinking.

Mid-January 2012

More than anybody, Dr. John understood how hard all of this church news was on me. Having to leave the church premises—especially the rectory after all that work—was horrible, with all my memories of Bill there.

More and more, I wanted to be where Bill was.

I spent a session with Gregg talking about religion and dying. Gregg is aware of how strong a Catholic I am. He mentioned the scripture about "God never gives you more than you can handle," and I started sobbing, saying I had always held comfort in that scripture, but I had lost that now, because losing Bill was the largest thing I couldn't handle. I had begun to wonder whether God was testing my faith.

January 29, 2012

We had the last Mass at St. Edmund's old location. Dave and Jaci met me there. Julie had tried to come, but the snow had kept her home. I was worried about whether I'd be able to hold it together, but I didn't need to worry—everyone was crying.

The trouble was, I kept crying later... and drinking.

Early February 2012

Life was so unbearable. Most of my thoughts were of Bill... but not the happy memories. Unfortunately, most of my thoughts were still of the accident and hospital time. I constantly remembered the moments before Bill died, watching blood dripping from his ear. Some of that blood had gotten on my hands and face. I think I remembered these moments so clearly because it was the last I had of Bill on this earth, the last time I could talk to him and hold him.

I prayed that when I died, I'd be in heaven with Jesus, Bill, and all my loved ones... and all other souls.

Monday, February 13, 2012

Father Russ paid me another visit. I started talking about the discussion we had last time he was at my house—about praying. Faith had become more intense in my life since I lost Bill. Father Russ reminded me that God needs to be the center of our world. He is the one that our focus should always be on. He is the reason we should want to go to heaven. It is His will that we should be following.

I knew all these things, but I had trouble focusing on Jesus when I missed Bill so much. I had to remember that I could still love Bill, as long as I remembered to also love Jesus.

I missed Bill so badly that most days I couldn't stand it… so I continued to pray to God for things of my will, not necessarily God's will. But I was trying. And trying. And trying.

Keys Day, Wednesday, February 15, 2012

This one really hit me. Thank goodness I had an appointment with Dr. John. I completely fell apart, telling him this all has to stop. I could see his concern. He discussed admitting me into the hospital, or joining the half-day hospital program.

I knew he was doing some serious thinking about my situation, but I fought it for now, and I said no.

I went home and started drinking again.

Friday, February 17, 2012

During my appointment with Gregg, he let me know that Dr. John had sent him a message. He also very strongly suggested I be admitted to the hospital or the half-day program. Once again, I fought it and said no.

He said my depression was worsening, and that I needed to get to the next step; he agreed I couldn't keep doing this. He said I'd need to give some thought to this.

I knew with Dr. John and Gregg both pushing me to go into the hospital or the half-day program, I'd end up doing one or the other. But I just wasn't ready. Or more truthfully, I was scared.

I couldn't imagine the next step unless it meant being in heaven with God and Bill.

Sunday, February 19, 2012

Back home from Church, I continued to think about what Dr. John and Gregg had been saying to me last week. *Was I too scared to listen to them? To anyone?* I wondered.

It's been one-and-a-half years since I lost my husband, Bill. It seemed like yesterday to me. Every day I think about the same things… over and over. *Why did the accident happen? Why was it Bill? Why did God want Bill so soon?* I questioned myself and God. I never blamed God, nor thought that he was punishing Bill. Bill was a good person and a good Christian. I felt maybe I had been missing—or ignoring—the secrets that God now shared with Bill.

The circumstances have changed me. I also see myself as a good person and a good Christian. And my situation has strengthened my devotion to God. It is more clear and precise than it was before. God is a much stronger focus in my everyday life. *How can he not be?* I ask myself daily. He has the answers to all my questions. He is where I want to be.

I know Bill is in heaven with God. And I hope that someday I will be able to join them. But I haven't yet found the patience to wait quietly. I struggle, hoping that every day is my last day.

I need to find out what God wants of me in this world. *What is my reason for staying here? And is that something that I should be contemplating in the first place?* I ask myself. I was back to thinking about whose will I should be following. I knew the answer every time I questioned it.

I'm struggling to live in a world that doesn't fit me anymore. I'm now nervous in crowds. I can't stand the noise in grocery stores as people plan their activities. I'm not concerned about the latest fashions, the newest restaurant, or getting new furniture. Instead, I spend my time wondering what God's plans are for me. I try to think of ways that I can help others who are hurting like me. Maybe that could be the fit I'm looking for.

So I know I still have a lot to learn.

I turned to reading the Bible, going to Bible study group, and praying. The Bible study group turned out to be an invaluable tool in showing me God's whole plan. A plan we are to follow. A plan that I still need to better understand.

And I've learned I'm not going to get my questions answered yet. *So what do I do?* I wonder.

I continue to see my psychiatrist and therapists to help me get through each day. I take my medications prescribed by my doctor. Their helpful interactions in my life decisions are invaluable to me. I'm now contemplating a stay in the psychiatric hospital. I see it as a time of respite, a time to slow down and listen to others around me who also feel their world is in an uproar.

I'm trying to accept more invitations from loving family and friends, to build a life with them—without Bill.

I go to church on Sundays and visit the cemetery afterwards to include Bill.

Like the swan that Father Sam talked about in his eulogy at Bill's service, I plan on waiting for the day that I am again with my mate.

And, very importantly, I read the Bible… I have learned in my reading that there are many references made regarding widows. What a joy to understand that God puts us in such high regard, and puts us in His protection.

***

The following is a list of my favorite passages from Psalms that hopefully will warm the hearts of other widows:

Psalm 23:6 – Sure goodness and mercy shall follow me all the days of my life, and I will dwell in the house of the LORD forever.

Psalm 27:14 – Wait on the LORD: be of good courage, and he shall strengthen thine heart: wait, I say, on the LORD.

Psalm 30:2 – O LORD, my God, I cried unto thee, and thou hast healed me.

Psalm 30:5 – For his anger endureth but a moment; in his favor is life: weeping may endure for a night, but joy cometh in the morning.

Psalm 34:18 – The LORD is nigh unto them that are of a broken heart; and saveth such as be of a contrite spirit.

Psalm 37:4 – Delight thyself also in the LORD; and he shall give thee the desires of thine heart.

Psalm 86:7 – In the day of my trouble I will call upon thee: for thou wilt answer me.

Psalm 107:9 – For he satisfieth the longing soul, and filleth the hungry soul with goodness.

And a selection of scriptures throughout the Bible:

Ecclesiastes 3:1,2,4 – To every thing there is a season, and a time to every purpose under the heaven: A time to be born, and a time to die; a time to plant, and a time to pluck up that which is planted; A time to weep, and a time to laugh; a time to mourn, and a time to dance;

Isaiah 1:17 – Learn to do well, seek judgment, relieve the oppressed, judge the fatherless, plead for the widow.

Matthew 11:28 – Come unto me, all ye that labour and are heavy laden, and I will give you rest.

Peter 5:7 – Casting all your care upon him; for he careth for you.

Proverbs 3:5 – Trust in the LORD with all thine heart, and lean not unto thine own understanding.

Romans 15:13 – Now the God of hope fill you with all joy and peace in believing, that ye may abound in hope, through the power of the Holy Ghost.

THE END

About the Author

Jean Kaiserling is a Wisconsin resident who knows how to deal with cold winters—she spends a great deal of time enjoying her home's lush, perennial gardens in the springtime of the year. She takes comfort in a close relationship with God, as she talks with Him daily; but more importantly, she *listens* to Him.

The idea for Jean's first book, *I Know You Love Me: To My Husband, Bill* came quickly, as she began writing journal entries about losing her husband, Bill. Then, she realized the details were something more than just journal entries—they were a journey—through the life and love she shared with Bill.

Jean hopes her journey through the Valley of the Shadow of Death will bring comfort to others.

www.ingramcontent.com/pod-product-compliance
Lightning Source LLC
Chambersburg PA
CBHW021636120626
46545CB00002B/567